# The Black Entrepreneur's Guide to Success

## Melvin J. Gravely, II

*a publication of*
*Duncan & Duncan, Inc.,*
*Publishers*

Edited by Apryl Motley

Library of Congress Catalog Card Number: 95-67017

Gravely, II, Melvin J.,
The Black Entrepreneur's Guide to Success

1. African-American business enterprises  2. Small business-Reference  3. Businesses - for African-Americans  4. Success  5. Afro-Americans, economic conditions
Index, Bibliography, Glossary, Appendix

ISBN  1-878647-23-7

Duncan & Duncan, Inc.
*Publishers*
Mailing address: P.O. Box 1137, Edgewood, MD 21040
Phone 410-538-5580   Fax  410-538-5584

This book is not a substitute for professional advice from a qualified business or legal practitioner. Duncan & Duncan, Inc. is not engaged in rendering business, legal or other professional counseling and cannot be held responsible for any loss incurred as a result of the application of any information in this publication. The reader should seek such professional advice when necessary.

10-9-8-7-6-5-4-3-2

# DISCARD

## *Dedication*

To my grandmothers—
*Louise Cotton and Roseanna Gravely*

# *Acknowledgments*

*T*o my loving and supportive wife Chandra, thank you for pushing me to finally go after this dream. You endured all of the long hours I spent at the computer completing this work. Your total support throughout this project made the difference. I owe its success to you.

To my daughter Cheree', thank you for understanding why dad needed to work such long hours. Thank you for being patient in waiting to do some of the fun things you wanted to do. You, as much as anyone, deserve credit for your role in the completion of this book.

To my parents Melvin Sr. and Sarah Gravely, thank you for all of your support and encouragement on this project and throughout my entire life.

To my only sister Jewel, despite having a husband and three young children, you found the time to spend many hours reviewing this book.

To my grandmothers Roseanna Gravely and Louise Cotton, it is your lives of perseverance and fortitude that continually motivate me. Thank you.

To Bob Wallace, for all of your advice and guidance in the writing of this book.

**To the dedicated individuals who agreed to read this manuscript well before it was ready to be published,** you all freely gave of your time and I will always be grateful: Tracy Veal Booker, Robert Crump III, Kendra Nordquist, John and Rosalind Webb, Wanda Young, and Dorien Nunez.

**To my life long friend and fraternity brother Brian Matthews,** whenever I really need to hear the truth, you are always there.

To all of the many people who gave me encouraging words and input that made this book possible, to the many small business owners who gave me interviews, I wish you all continued success. Never give up on your dreams. Thank you all and God bless.

*Mel Gravely, II*

*6*

# Table of Contents

# *Foreword*

*M* el Gravely II, author of *The Black Entrepreneur's Guide to Success*, has been able to capture the **steps to business ownership** in this comprehensive book. Mel covers everything from preparing yourself, to getting started, to creating a sellable product, and to keeping the customers you get. This book is full of interesting stories, examples, and real world tips presented in an effort to make you more confident, prepared, and aware. Mel's no excuses approach to business is one that will motivate you to positive action toward the realization of your goals.

The media is full of negative press about the black business community. What they often fail to tell you is that black-owned firms fared better than their majority-owned counterparts during the recession of the early 1990s. As a matter of fact, in 1992 when many white-owned auto dealerships were laying people off, black-owned dealerships had their best year ever. Do not believe the press. African-Americans do have what it takes to succeed in business.

*The Black Entrepreneur's Guide to Success* gives you the answer to how you personally can get what you want from your business. In basic, everyday language, Mel takes you through the process. Real life examples bring the concepts to life.

Our quest to own more business enterprises is important. *The Wall Street Journal* studied government labor figures and found that during the 1990/91 recession, some large corporations shed black workers disproportionately. As a matter of fact, African-Americans were the only cultural group to have a net loss in jobs during this time frame. This points to a need for more black-owned businesses. Since African-American firms tend to hire more African-Americans, entrepreneurship in the black community will give our community more stable jobs. It will also mean better role models and a generally higher standard of living.

Our community is already a force to deal with. We account for three hundred billion dollars of income per year. According to retail-industry statistics, American women in general each spend an average of seven hundred to eight hundred dollars a year for clothing. African-American women each spend an average of eleven hundred dollars a year. We are making more money. We simply must have more quality African-American businesses in which to spend it. In *The Black Entrepreneur's Guide to Success*, Mel Gravely II motivates you to be one of the individuals who will get your business started now.

When I started my first business in the late 1960s, networking was informal. As our communities have grown, organizations like SuccessSource have moved networking to a new level of effectiveness. We can now bring more individuals together who can really help each other be more successful. I call it "doing well by doing good." In the late sixties, my growing network was all I had. I quickly realized the value that effective networking can bring.

Mel is quickly becoming known for "doing well by doing good." His corporate, entrepreneurial, and networking background all come out in this easy to read book for business success. I believe this book can make the difference for you. Read the book, internalize the concepts, and get started. African-American entrepreneurs everywhere await your entry into business ownership!

George Fraser
Author, *Success Runs In Our Race*

# *Introduction*

*"Black folks need to blow out the dim lamp of poverty and turn on the beacon light of hope."*
—T.J. Jemison, President,
National Baptist Convention

## *Why Is There a Need for Black Entrepreneurship?*

*T*he black entrepreneur along with the black church has been the cornerstone of the black community since the end of slavery. Businesses like blacksmiths, shoe repair shops, barbers, beauticians, farmers, restaurants, cocktail lounges, and law offices are all examples of a history of black entrepreneurship. Black business owners have been able to survive in the most oppressive of situations. Black entrepreneurs give the African-American community ownership of our future.

My paternal grandmother always preached ownership as a way of controlling the future. She struggled for years cleaning the homes of the rich, an occupation called "day work". Before dawn, she would catch the bus from her poor black neighborhood across town to large homes owned by the city's elite residents. Blind in one eye and limited in formal education, my grandmother sold her skills to enough white families to raise three children alone. She worked long hours doing laundry, scrubbing floors and taking care of her employer's children.

My grandmother was proud doing work few of us would consider doing today. She still boasts of the quality of her superior abilities in the domestic area. Although I have used cleaners all over the United States, no one can launder a cotton shirt as well as my grandma Rose.

After years of day work, my grandmother finally got a chance to own her own destiny. She rented a concession stand on the first floor of the county court house and became her own boss. She probably doesn't realize it, but she was our family's first entrepreneur. My grandma's business serviced the needs of her customers for years. She was always there with coffee, donuts, candy, and polite conversation. My grandmother inspired me to want to control my situation. She often talked about sacrifice and dependability.

Just like my grandmother, black entrepreneurs around the country serve as role models for self determination. Business owners also provide needed jobs and financial support for our community. Working in corporate America can be a great occupation. I spent much of my career with IBM, and many of my friends still work in the corporate environment.

But black entrepreneurs signify freedom and independence. Whether you plan to run your business part-time or full-time is not what is important. Just as my grandmother was critical to my personal development, black entrepreneurship is vital to the future of our community.

# Why Is This the Right Time for Black Businesses?

The climate is right for African-American businesses. It is time for African- American business owners to get their piece of the economic pie. There are five reasons for my assertion that now is the best time since slavery for blacks to start businesses. The first and most significant reason is the large amount of money that African-Americans generate in income and spend on products and services.

In his book, *Success Runs In Our Race*, George Fraser points out our race generates three hundred billion dollars a year in income. We represent the fourteenth largest economy in the industrialized world. We also tend to spend a higher percentage of our income than the average for all Americans.

For example, Fraser quotes retail-industry statistics that show African-American women spend four to five hundred dollars a year more than the female population in general. Although a U.S. Census Bureau study shows the number of black businesses are growing at 38% a year, there are not enough companies making enough products to supply the purchasing desires of the black community.

Second, we have more African-Americans in positions of influence and decision-making than ever before. From the White House to corporate America, African-Americans are finally moving into positions of significant power. With more blacks in key positions, African-American business owners can rely on relationships that never existed before. For example, there are more black mayors of major cities than at anytime in our history.

In recent history, major cities like Cleveland, Atlanta, Detroit, Washington, Cincinnati, Minneapolis, and Denver have now or have had black mayors. This country has more black congress and cabinet members than ever before. Vernon

Jordan led the transition team for President Bill Clinton and remains one of the President's close personal advisors. These relationships will improve African-American business owners' access to the billions of dollars of business done by our nations businesses and government agencies.

Third, top business talent is more readily available to African-American businesses. As large corporations continue to reduce their staff levels, outstanding business people are now available to black businesses. This additional talent pool will allow minority businesses to add trained professionals to their personnel. Better employees will position our businesses to perform better quality services and provide higher quality products. These people will bring the expensive training and development of large corporations to the small business environment.

Fourth, more and more, large corporations and government agencies are recognizing the value of doing business with African-American businesses. Government agencies are aggressively trying to align the amount of money spent with minority businesses and the minority population of the area. Cities like Cleveland and Detroit have set-aside as much as 30% of total dollars spent by the city to be spent with minority-owned businesses. (Programs that earmark a percentage of business to be done with minority-owned companies are called minority set-asides. This term will be used throughout this book.)

Private industry also recognizes the value of doing business with African-Americans. Many large corporations have established aggressive minority purchasing objectives. These objectives are being raised each year as the corporations become more comfortable purchasing goods and services from minority businesses. Most of the nation's largest firms have put together special programs to find quality minority vendors that can add value to the products and services of the large company.

Finally, I feel positive about the present climate for black businesses because of the existence of special programs that really help the development of African-American businesses. Special programs for minority businesses have been available for many years, but few of the programs really got to the root of the problems facing minority businesses. In the past few years, new loan, technical assistance, and set-aside programs have been developed by people who have a better understanding of the minority business. These new programs are designed to really assist minority business development.

More economic spending power, high-level contacts, the availability of higher quality personnel, a new recognition of the value of black businesses, and new innovative programs means that **now** is the best time ever to start your business.

## Why This Book?

This book was written because I wish that this information would have been available when I started my first business. Although I read many of the popular small business books available, none of them gave the "real life" perspective for a black-owned business. I always wondered about the special issues facing black business owners. What do our businesses have to do differently to be successful? No one should have to learn through the trial and error method that I and many others were forced to use.

I remember being invited to an interview for the opportunity to perform services for a small city in northeast Ohio. It was our first interview as a company and we were excited about the chances of this meeting turning into an actual job. The project was a minority set-aside, so we were in competition with four other minority companies. We presented our company and why we felt we were the best selection for this project. After we finished our presentation, the city manager began asking questions along these lines: Is this the only business you are involved in? You're not involved in real-estate or anything else? We were puzzled by his questions. After months of running our business, the reason for the city manager's questions became clear. He had a poor image of minority businesses. He thought we were all in business just to take advantage of special programs and make quick money. He had no concept of the idea that a minority business is simply a business owned by persons from a minority group.

None of the books I had read prepared me for this type of mind-set. Not one book even touched on the image of African-American businesses. Having this information before the interview would have prepared me to show this city manager enough to erase his concerns. As it turned out, we did not get the business because we were not prepared to address the issues.

This step-by-step guide for building a business was written to help African-Americans recognize and overcome common barriers. **It combines information from many sources and presents it from an African-American perspective.** Included are examples of real situations that you will face and insight on how you can overcome them. It is a fact that African-American businesses are not competing on an even playing field, **but this lack of equality is no excuse for failing in business. My book is a guide to working within the system to be sure your business is successful.**

## How to Get the Most from This Book?

To get the most from this book, you should first answer a primary question. Are you a business technician or a business entrepreneur? Some businesses are started for the sole purpose of creating a job for the business owner. These business owners are what are called business technicians. Business technicians are in business to do what ever it is the business does. The plumber who owns a plumbing business concentrates on the plumbing portion of the business. These owners usually care little about growth, employees, or business systems. The business provides the plumber a job and the good feeling of owning his own business.

Other businesses are started with the goal of creating wealth. These businesses may or may not be established by people who can perform the work of the business. Restaurants are many times started by people who can not cook and do not want to wait tables. These wealth-building business owners are called entrepreneurs. They focus on the business side of the business. Entrepreneurs are focused on business growth. To a business entrepreneur, every business is the same. Each business needs marketing, management, financing, and business systems.

Both business technicians and business entrepreneurs are important and can be successful. The key is to know which type of business you have and which type you want. A major reason for the high number of business failures in general, and African-American businesses specifically, is because of business owners not making the distinction between the two types of operations.

This book focuses on subjects that will assist both types of businesses. The content gives you the tools that you need to assess the type of business you are in. Then, you will be able to make the transition from technician to entrepreneur and vice versa. Transition involves focusing on the business of the business and understanding the impact of growth on you and your business.

Long-term survival depends on our ability to successfully grow strong businesses. Throughout the chapters that follow, I use the terms business owner and entrepreneur interchangeably to identify all types of business operators. Find yourself and your business in this writing, and applying these concepts will be simple.

The book is separated into seven parts. Read each part in

order. Do not try to take notes or highlight information as you read it through the first time. Simply read through the material to get a general understanding of the content. Use the business glossary in the back of the book to look up the definitions of any words or subjects with which you are not familiar. Some sections may not appear to pertain to your business. Read these sections also. You may learn new concepts that can be translated into to your purposes.

After reading the entire book through once, you are ready to take notes. Read through the book again. Only read the sections that you believe pertain to your business. Take notes and highlight material in the book. Try some of the concepts and return to the book for more detail. Keep the book handy to refresh your memory on particular subjects. For example, if you are about to make a sales call, review the section of the book that gives you tips on making effective sales calls. Use the book as a tool to give you answers to everyday business questions. Write in it, fold down pages, and use your highlighter. It is your book. Get the most from it.

*Mel Gravely*

# Part I: Preparing Yourself

Preparing yourself for the exciting journey of running your own business will require considerable thought. Sharpening your entrepreneurial skills, fighting procrastination, preparing your family, and keeping yourself motivated will all need your attention. Give yourself the time needed to get these issues in place. **You are the base of your business.** Create a strong foundation, and the house you build will last a long time.

_____ *1*

# Common Traits of Entrepreneurship

*"Most people search high and wide for the keys to success.*
*If they only knew, the key to their dreams lies within."*
—George Washington Carver

*P* reparing yourself to be a successful entrepreneur requires that you understand the make-up of a prosper-
ous business owner. African-Americans often believe it takes
mythical traits to start and run a business. Advanced education, rich parents and superior intellect are the traits cited
most by non-business people. Although there has been much
study of this subject, no one has determined the exact for-
mula for becoming a successful entrepreneur.

Research from various sources has revealed what I call
the **Final Four of Entrepreneurship** (Figure 1.1). These four
traits are the most commonly mentioned, referred to and
depended on by business owners. **Although these traits cross
racial lines, their level of intensity and importance is greater
for the black business owner.**

Understand and internalize these traits, and you will have
taken the first step in preparing yourself to own a successful
business.

The first of the *final four* of entrepreneurship is **guts**. When I was still working for IBM, a colleague and friend asked me a question that changed my perception of what it takes to be a success in business: "If you had to choose between having brains or having guts, which would you choose?" Maybe the answer to this question should have been easy, but it took me several minutes to answer.

I always thought brains would take you anywhere you wanted to go. But as I thought about the people I revered for their accomplishments in business, it was their guts that made them different. If you think about it, few of the top business people in the world created the products their companies produce. If they are not the brains behind the product, why are they in charge? Why do they own the ideas? Why are they the most rewarded? Because they have the guts. It really is that simple.

**Successful business owners have the guts to start the company, make the decisions and live with the results.** Don't believe that entrepreneurs are born with guts. Most entrepreneurs build their level of confidence as they develop their business. Formulation of a solid business idea and a thorough business plan gives potential business owners the confidence to go for their dream.

There is a reason guts is the first of the final four of entrepreneurship. **Having guts is the most important of the final four for the African-American entrepreneur.** Your road to running a successful business is cluttered with institutionally created obstacles that you have no control over. It will take guts to challenge the system and move your business ideas forward.

The second of the *final four* is **vision**. **Vision is the entrepreneur's mental picture of what the business will be.** Vision is the guiding light that directs the activities of your company. Vision can also be a motivater. If you can see the mental picture of your objectives, it will be easier to take

**Figure 1.1. The Final Four of Entrepreneurship**

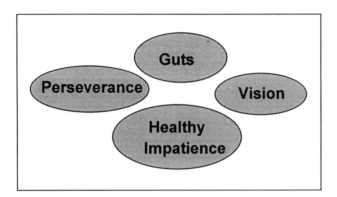

actions toward their fulfillment. Great leaders have the ability to transfer their vision to others and gain support for pursuit of this vision. Entrepreneurs with a strong vision can see their company, its products and its position in the market place. With vision, a business owner will be able to plan for long-term performance.

I met an African-American entrepreneur at a small business conference a few years ago. As we talked about our individual businesses, it was evident that this young man had a clear vision: "I want to be 12 million-dollar company in ten years," he said. "We plan to grow through new product developments and aggressive acquisitions," he continued.

His most persuasive statement was "we use technology better than anyone else in our industry. That is our competitive advantage." Without knowing what business this black business owner was in, I already knew a lot about it. He had simply shared his vision with me.

Think about your business yesterday, today, and tomorrow and decide where you see yourself going. Your vision should be clear, concise and repeated often. All of your employees should understand the vision. Yes, your vision can change over time, but without a vision you will always struggle to establish and maintain the identity of your business.

The third aspect of the *final four* is **healthy impatience**. **Healthy impatience is a feeling that good things need to be done sooner.** I can't remember where I heard it first, but it is the single statement my daughter hates the most: "If something is worth doing, it is worth doing sooner." I say it all the time. It is really a basic thought.

If you were going to receive $100,000 and you were given the option of receiving the money now or 10 years from now, which would you choose? Of course we would all choose to receive the money now. Since the $100,000 has value, it is worth having sooner. So is the case in business. Tomorrow is never soon enough for a good idea. Take this approach and you will always push your good ideas forward. You will receive the benefits of these ideas earlier and stay ahead of your competition.

As others see your approach, they will respond by treating you and your business with a sense of urgency. What you are doing will always be important to others.

Healthy impatience is not being pushy. It is an attitude of progress. Healthy impatience is moving forward toward your goals and objectives. Moving through obstacles, over roadblocks and around people who don't understand how important it is you succeed.

**Perseverance** is the last of the final four of entrepreneurship. **It is the last because it is the toughest of the four to put into practice.** Begin by setting aggressive but realistic goals. Instant success does not happen often. You should expect a slow start-up period. Your company will have little or no track record. You may also be lacking in personal credibility. It will be tough to convince your first customer to give you the chance you need.

In his book *Black Wealth Through Black Entrepreneurship,*

Robert Wallace calls it the "first hit" phenomenon. The first hit phenomenon says that black entrepreneurs struggle for quite some time before they get their first significant customer. After this "first hit," the entrepreneur's business has some credibility. The business now has a small track record to reference for other clients. The "first hit" is a significant step in the development of the minority business, but you have to persevere long enough to get there. Never give up on your dreams.

**If your plan is good, continue to work it. If your present approach is not working, try a different approach. But whatever you decide, don't quit.** Thousands of failed entrepreneurs quit the day before they would have received their "first hit." You will have to rebound from people saying "no" to your business. You may get "no's" from the bank, private investors and your potential customers. Remember every no only puts you closer to your first yes. Your "yes" may be on your next telephone call. Persevere and never quit.

These are the proven traits of the most successful entrepreneurs in this country. Many debate whether entrepreneurs are born or made. Since all four of these key traits can be developed and enhanced, it is possible that entrepreneurs are both born and made. Knowing the traits is the first step. Keep these traits in mind as you continue to build your business. Review this section often. Read related business books to increase your general business knowledge and your confidence with business concepts.

Make sure your business plan is complete and read it on a regular basis. Surround yourself with other successful minority business owners. They can share in your experiences and renew your confidence in the value of owning your own company. Remember, you are the business. Invest in yourself and you will be investing in your business.

2

# *Getting Started—Fighting Procrastination*

*"There aren't really enough crutches in the world for all the lame excuses."*
> —Bill Demby,
> Physically Challenged Athlete &
> Motivational Speaker

*W*hile you are preparing yourself to really grow your business, **you must gain control over procrastination.** People procrastinate for many different reasons. The most frequent reasons are fear of failure or success, depression, shyness, inadequate information, hopelessness, and fatigue.

These situations occur due to years and years of oppression, frustration, and disappointment. The black community suffers from these conditions more than others. **Our cultural history has caused a feeling of dependency—dependence on a system that has never had our best interests in mind.** These conditions have paralyzed many blacks.

Research has shown that the best way to break through

your desire to put things off is to break the task down to smaller parts. Looking at a project as a whole will make the project appear too large and overwhelming. You may not know what to do first. Consider slicing the project like a salami. By cutting the project into smaller pieces it will be more inviting to pick up and take a bite. While the project is in one piece it is unappetizing, hard and crusty like a large piece of uncut salami.

Make a list of the tasks needed to complete the project. Be sure to break the steps down into single tasks. For example, looking into what is needed to become incorporated is not a single task. A task associated with this step may be calling the state attorney general's office for the needed paperwork.

Some people believe you should perform the easy tasks first. Doing the easy tasks first will help you build momentum that will carry you through the project. Objects in motion tend to stay in motion. This basic law of physics is true for your business activities as well.

Another strategy is for you to do the most difficult items first. You will then have the toughest part of the project complete and the rest of the project will be easy. Still others believe you should attack the tasks in the order that makes the most sense. Certain steps logically come before others. This method requires you to understand how the steps fit together. **My experience has shown your approach to handling the list of tasks is not important. The important thing is action.** You must be willing to take action to start and complete each task. There is no substitute for self-motivation. At some point, the future of your business will be up to you.

A new business owner in the Midwest, we will call him Tim, was ready to start marketing his product. He had secured his supplier and negotiated a price low enough to guarantee a sufficient profit margin. Tim came to me for assistance in preparing a marketing program. We have been personal friends for many years and it was a pleasure to be able to assist him. We discussed multiple options to market and distribute his innovative product. After our discussions, he was confident he could complete and implement the plan. The offer was extended for him to call me with any other questions.

Two months passed and I contacted Tim to determine his progress. He said he needed to sit down and spend the time needed to document his marketing plan. He explained how busy he had been and how much he really wanted this business to work. During our conversation, he talked about his trips to Canada, Atlanta, and Los Angeles. In the two months time since we had last spoken, he had taken three personal "mini" vacations. There was nothing more I could say. Tim had an understanding of what he needed to do. He would have to make the decision to do it.

Action is the key. Get the project started, and you will be surprised how momentum will continue to carry you through. **One last tip is to set aggressive but realistic deadlines for completion of each task. Aggressive but realistic means setting a date and time that will make you have to work hard but will not put you under unnecessary strain.** You decide on what the deadline will be, but setting a deadline is a must.

A would be entrepreneur, we will call Louise, contacted me for assistance in developing a business plan. She asked me to send her a copy of my detailed business plan outline. We talked a few months later to discuss her business ideas. She was not sure what business she wanted to start.  We talked of potential ideas based on her particular skills and interest. I urged her to set some objectives and deadlines for the development of her ideas. She attended one of our firms small business seminars to continue to gather information for her future business. She continued to talk about starting a business for the next year. She always had a good reason why now was not a good time to begin: "As soon as I finish this project at work" or "When I get myself together I will be ready to get started."

My grandfather, the late Reverend William H. Cotton, pastor of Peoples' Baptist Church, Canton, Ohio, always made it clear: "If you are waiting for the perfect time, that time is now." He was talking about accepting God's salvation, but the message is the same for starting your business. As of the printing of this book, Louise still has not started her business. She has not investigated any specific business idea. She is in a war with procrastination and self doubt. Her only hope is to use action as a weapon and begin to fight back.

3

# *Preparing Your Family*

*"Where there is no vision........"* the people perish
—Proverbs 29:18

*T*he family unit is the center of the African-American community. **The family is a critical part of the success of any black business owner.** You will need the support of your loved ones in order to continue giving your business the attention it will need to grow. Since your family will play such a significant role, it is important to understand what impact your business may have on your family. Starting your own business could impact your love ones in three major ways:

**1) Starting a business may effect your family financially.** If you are planning to operate your business full-time, you will need to be sure your family will be provided for. Do you have enough savings? **Most financial experts suggest at least 18 months of income in savings.** Is your spouse able to handle the household bills? What is your emergency plan if your financial projections are incorrect? If your household income is going to drop due to your business, you need to make sure the family is aware. Get their commitment to your goals and objectives. Unless you are independently wealthy, your family will have to learn to live with less—less to spend on dining out, less for new clothing purchases, and less for new homes or new cars.

After running our engineering company part-time for three years, we decided that it was time to make the move to full-time entrepreneurship. Our business plan and financial projections showed that we would be able to afford to pay myself and my partner a moderate salary. Combined with the salary of our wives, we felt we could maintain our current standard of living. Unfortunately our projections were off.

We made our move to run our business full-time the fall before the worst Ohio winter in twenty-five years. The extreme weather not only delayed two major projects but halted three that were already underway. This situation immediately dried up revenue. We went from twenty thousand dollars of revenue per month to seven thousand dollars.

From the months of November through March, we suffered. For many months my partner and I had to come home and explain to our wives why we were not going to get a paycheck. Our wives were understanding and very supportive. If the situation had been different, I may have had to give up my business and return to working for someone else. Prepare your family for the worst. Be honest about your plans and gain their complete support. Their sacrifices won't last forever. When your business is a success, your family will also reap the benefits.

**Don't believe that a part-time business will have less of an impact on your family's financial position. The financial needs of a part-time business can eat up all of the excess income from your full-time job.** This shift in financial priorities can catch your family off guard. Share your plans with your family. Let them know what changes to expect. The financial impact can be great but it does not have to be disastrous. Sharing your entire plan will help your family gain confidence that their sacrifices are worth it.

**2) Your business will also place more demands on your personal time.** If your business is to be a success, it will require a great deal of your time. Your children and spouse must be sold on your idea. They must understand and commit themselves to the success of the business. If time becomes a problem, there are some things you can do to help.

Have set hours you will spend with your family. I suggest after school for the children. Set this time aside and make it for the family. Be as committed to this time as you are to the business. Your family will see your effort and respect your commitment. This will make it easier to get their support when you are working on weekends and late nights. Don't forget your spouse. Take long weekends and romantic nights. Your family is your biggest and most powerful investor. If they withdraw their support, you and your business will suffer.

**3) The impact of  your business on your state of mind will also effect your family**. Your attention will be split in a million directions. The entrepreneurial mind rarely takes a break from business. My wife often reminds me of our evening out at a Will Downing concert. To this day I cannot remember how my mind drifted away from the concert and on to business. But my wife looked over at me in the middle of *I Try* and asked "What are you thinking about?"

My mind had left the concert. I was thinking about a new market our company wanted to enter. On a Saturday evening, at an outstanding concert with my wife and friends, I was thinking about business. Owning your own business is not like having a regular job. Your business will occupy your mind. The mind of a business owner is the business' most overworked tool.  You should expect to be thinking about business often. Explain to your family why your mind may wonder from time to time. Your mind will go through many ups and downs as your business grows. Make your family aware of your struggles and through understanding, they will be prepared to support you.

**Finances, time, and state of mind are the three ways that your business will affect your family.** Be mindful of this and always keep your family involved. They are your anchor, and their support is important. You can have a solid family life and a successful business. Making it work will take planning, sacrifice, and understanding.

4
_____

# Keeping Yourself Motivated

*"Let us lay aside every weight....and let us run with patience the race that is set before us."*

—Hebrew 12:1

*T*he **state of mind** of an entrepreneur is very important. Since your mind is the only thing you have complete control over, it is critical to use it as a powerful tool to help you succeed in business. Your mind, just like your body, can be exercised to keep it in top working order. Keeping your mind in shape will give you a competitive advantage over your competition. You will be more enthused, more personable, and more accepted. The following key strategies will help you keep your business mind in shape.

**Surround yourself with positive people.** Establish relationships with people who feel good about themselves and their opportunities. Look for people you think are positive and committed to success. We all know life is full of obstacles, tragedy and negative people. You will face rejection and failures as you attempt to grow your business enterprise. We all must carry our portion of the burdens of our negative world.

The difference between your success and your failure lies in your ability to deal with the negative situations with a positive attitude. Negative people will attract negative outcomes and will drain your energy. Positive people get positive outcomes and inspire you to do great things.

**Fill your mind with positive information.** Reading motivational books and magazines is a good way to keep yourself motivated. *Think and Grow Rich, A Black Choice* by Dennis Kimbro is a motivational book aimed at African-Americans. The book chronicles various African-Americans who reached success through the power of their thinking. Magazines such as *Ebony, Black Enterprise, Success,* and *Inc.* profile individuals and groups who have found much success in business. You can find a list of suggested reading material in Appendix B of this book.

The key is to continue to read about African-Americans who have succeeded. These success profiles will help you believe that you too can succeed. You can often get good ideas for your business or personal life from reading these publications. You might also want to consider listening to motivational audio tapes.

Speakers such as Les Brown produce tapes designed to give you tips that motivate you to reach your full potential. The advantage of audio tapes is that you can listen to them while driving in your car or sitting in your office. Many motivational books are also available on  audio tapes.

**Set realistic goals.** Set your expectations high but make sure they are achievable. Set your goals based on the projections in your business plan. A good business plan will allow you to understand how well you should be doing at any point in the progress of your business. If your goals are out of line with what your business can actually do, you will perceive you are not doing well.

**A business grows through a series of cyclical wins and**

**losses.** Your business plan will keep you focused on your goals and objectives and not on individual deals. Celebrate the wins, cry over the losses, but keep your eyes on your realistic plan.

**Separate who you are from what you do.** Who you are should not be defined by your occupation or the success or failure of your business. You are a woman, a man, a mother, or a father. Keep in mind what is really important to you. **There are many peaks and valleys on your road to success. Focus on what is really important, and you will be able to continue to push your small business forward.** It is never good for **you** to become your business.

Following these simple tips will keep you motivated in your business enterprise. Controlling your state of mind will be important if you plan on successfully running a business. Spend time feeding your mind healthy things and positive information. You must always believe you can, will , and must succeed.

# Part II:
# Minding Your Business

The **level of effort** you put into forming your business will determine your chances for success. This section outlines a model that will help you do everything from creating a product to choosing the proper business structure. This is the actual business of doing business. Spend time reviewing the content of this section.

*5*

---

# *The Basic Business Process*

*Business is like riding a bicycle—either you keep moving or you fall down.*

—Anonymous

*P*reparing the business is as important as preparing yourself. Whether you've been in business for years or you are just getting started today, the **basic principles of business cannot be ignored.** Preparing your business is like adding structural support to the foundation of a new home. The effort you put into this support will dictate whether you are building the mansion of your dreams or an unstable tin shack. Investing your time now will make the difference between business success or failure.

Most black entrepreneurs follow the Nike shoe philosophy and "just do it." Generally, we don't spend enough time **planning** our business ventures? Businesses in our community are often on one extreme or another. Either we don't plan at all or we continue to plan forever without ever really starting a business. Planning is important and even more important to black businesses for three major reasons:

1) **We often have fewer dollars and therefore have less of an opportunity to recover from a business mistake.** For example, if we open our doors for business and have not done the correct marketing job, we could be out of money and out of business by the time we correct our mistake. A jazz club opened in my home town. All of the black middle-class, middle-aged residents were excited. They would finally have a safe place to relax and have a mature evening out.

Opening day was a major success. The new club owners had sent personal invitations to all of the black notables in the community. The turn out was strong and everyone had a good time. As weeks passed the crowd steadily fell off. Why? The black middle-class, middle-aged community did not go out every weekend. Due to the limited number of middle-aged jazz lovers in the community, they all would have had to come every weekend to make the club a success. The club was forced to change their format to a more widely accepted form of music.

This change to a hip-hop dance music format brought a younger clientele. Although the crowds grow slightly larger, the new format was a further turnoff to their original target market. The younger crowd wanted to spend less for drinks, and they rarely ordered food. Although the owners changed their format, they were no longer a jazz club for the black middle-aged market nor were they a real hip hop club. Their drinks were too expensive for clients in the new market and their business was structured to get profits from food sales. All of these changes hurt profits and caused the jazz club/ restaurant to close.

What happened to this business idea that appeared to be so good? What if the owners knew the size of their target market (middle-aged, middle-income blacks) was too small to support this type of business long-term? What if they had known that middle-aged, middle-income whites are also jazz lovers. Would their marketing strategy have been different? If they would have followed a systematic planning process, they would have been prepared to tap the true market potential. By the time the business owners recognized their error, they were out of money and therefore had no chance to recover.

2) **Planning will give your business needed credibility.** Most black businesses have a major image problem. We are all lumped into the category of short-term, poorly financed, poorly planned businesses. As you approach outside investors, banks, and potential customers, having a well thought out plan will improve your image. Time after time black business owners tell me stories of being "interrogated" about the structure of their business. Having the answers to any question about your business will begin to build your presence as a business person.

I remember meeting with a potential customer about an engineering project that they were considering. We were one of three companies being interviewed for the project. After spending some time talking about our experience with his type of project and the structure of our proposed project team, the conversation turned to the business side of our company.

He began to ask why we went into this business. Who was our target market? How did we plan to grow? How did we determine our pricing strategy? After we had answered a series of questions of this type it was evident what he was doing. We were a certified minority business enterprise (MBE), and he knew it. He had an image in his mind of what an MBE was (or was not). We had obviously done well during the interview. He was trying to find out whether we were real. He wondered if we were really running the company or were we simply a "front" for some large white firm? We must have satisfied his curiosity and his perception of our business because we got the job. Having a plan will improve your image and black businesses desperately need to improve their image.

**3) Planning allows you to test your business idea before spending money.** By using a systematic planning approach, you can actually run your business idea on paper. When General Motors develops a new car, they always make a prototype or model of the new car. GM wants to make sure that the engine fits under the hood and that the gears do not rub together. They are testing the vehicle to see if it works.

Just like your business idea, GM believes their new car will run, but they would never mass produce a car they had not modeled. **You too need to model your idea.** This is a low cost, low risk way to guarantee the soundness of what you believe is an outstanding business idea.

I spend a considerable amount of time driving in my car alone. This time is used to think of new business ideas. My portable tape recorder captures the ideas, and I send each idea through a quick review process. Some ideas quickly turn out not to be viable. Other ideas seem to have some potential. Then I send these ideas through a structured development model (Figure 5.1). Many options prove not to be viable while others seem to be sound business opportunities. The key is that I have spent no money to test drive the ideas, and I now know if the idea runs or if it is a clunker.

This model is the core agenda for Parts II, III, and IV of this book. It is highlighted here and will be fully explained in the chapters that follow. The model is a six step process in question form. The answers to these questions will be the structured plan that your business idea needs.

## The Basic Business Model

**Can you sell it?** Answering this first question requires

**Figure 5.1. Basic Business Model**

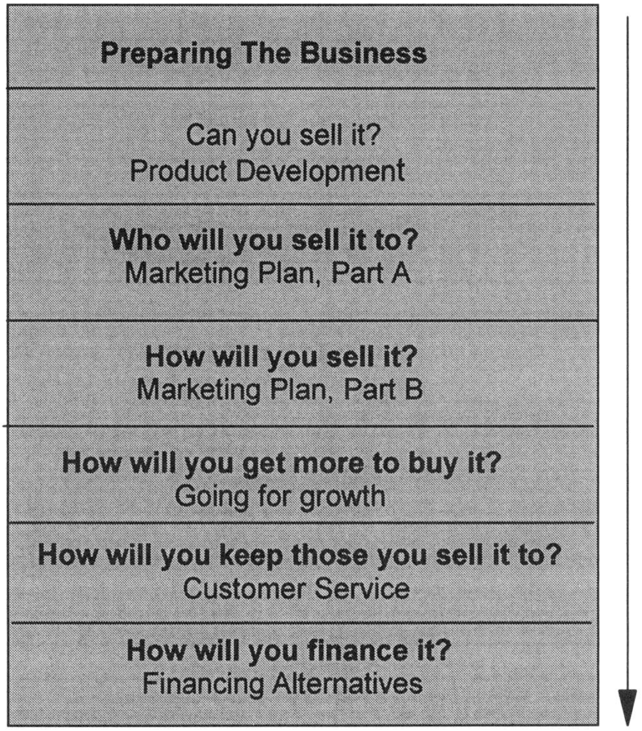

| |
|---|
| **Preparing The Business** |
| Can you sell it?<br>Product Development |
| **Who will you sell it to?**<br>Marketing Plan, Part A |
| **How will you sell it?**<br>Marketing Plan, Part B |
| **How will you get more to buy it?**<br>Going for growth |
| **How will you keep those you sell it to?**<br>Customer Service |
| **How will you finance it?**<br>Financing Alternatives |

that you look at your product or service to determine whether or not it can be sold. This section is commonly called product development. In this section, you will specifically define your product. You will go through a process to select the right product for you based on your interest, talents, finances, opportunities, and aspirations. You will establish the important traits of your product such as its' price, image, and competitive advantage.

**Who will you sell it to?** After you have determined the right product for your business, you will need to find someone to buy it. Throughout this section, you will determine your target market of potential customers. You will determine their population size, product desires and buying habits. I know this sounds like a lot of work but the model will guide you through it step-by-step. Most of the information is easy and inexpensive to find at your local library.

**How will you sell it?** In this section, you will develop strategies for getting your potential customers to buy your product or service. You will select the proper methods to inform your clients about your product. The model will guide your actions so that you use the advantages of your product and the buying habits of your target market to maximize your sales.

**How will you satisfy those who buy it?** Now that you have convinced people to buy your product, you must find a way to maintain them as satisfied customers. This is a question of customer service. The model will guide you in the development of a customer service system geared toward keeping your customers satisfied and coming back for life.

**How will you get more customers?** You have sold your product to customers and now have a plan to keep them satisfied. Now you are ready to start growing. I like to call it **going for growth**. This section gives you ideas on growing your business. You will find how you can build new products from old ones. You will also know how to create new services with your present skills. This section prepares you for issues associated with rapid growth. You will learn the importance of business systems and how to effectively implement them.

**How will you finance it?** Even the greatest ideas need money to bring them to life. You will evaluate methods of financing and determine the correct financing strategy for your business. Banks, private investors, venture capitalists, and self-financing are all discussed. Methods for increasing your chances of obtaining financing are also reviewed.

The chapters that follow discuss each of the sections of the basic business model outlined here in more detail. These chapters provide information that will help you translate your great business ideas into sound business practices.

6

---

# What Business Is Right for You?

*"Every new idea is an impossibility until it is born."*
—Ron Brown,
Secretary,
U.S. Department of Commerce

C hoosing the right product for your business is a step-by-step process. The selection process presented in this chapter will help you to systematiclly choose the products that best fit you, your environment, and the present situation. Think of this process as a type of sift. Ideas that do not fit you are caught by the system and discarded. Viable ideas pass through to the next step for further evaluation.

## The Five-Step Product Selection Process

**Step 1: Brainstorm.** Brainstorm for all and any business ideas. Brainstorming is the process of creating a list of ideas or thoughts. There is no pre-judgement of the ideas. You simply list all of the ideas that come to mind. As you try to come up with new ideas, think about your daily habits. What products do you use each day that could become your company's product? Do you ever hear people saying they hate to do something that you think is exciting? Could this be a business opportunity? What are you doing for a living now? Can you turn your present job into your new business? Consider offering support services for churches or other organizations. Read magazines like *Black Enterprise, Success,* and *Inc.* that often present interesting new businesses ideas. Look through advertisements for available franchise opportunities. Franchising can be a good business as well as a source of an idea for your new start up.

All ideas get listed. Remember you are brainstorming. There will be plenty of time to critique each idea later. Dream! The sky is the limit. Often the ideas you think are the most outrageous are the ideas that make you think of great business opportunities. Your ideas do not have to be unique. Just list the ideas and send them through this selection process.

**Step 2: Narrow your list.** Review your list of business ideas and cross out the obvious no-win selections. Be careful! If you are not sure about any idea, keep it for further review. You should not discard an idea just because you have no talent or knowledge in the area. When narrowing your business possibilities, consider yourself first.

**Measure each business idea based on two personal items: your interest in the business and your personal skills, strength, and background in the area.** If both your interest and your personal skills are high, the business opportunity moves to the next level. However, having high interest and low skill does not always count the idea out.

Can you hire the skill you need? Do you know enough about the business to make it a success? You must be honest through this process to assure you will get good results. Eliminate the ideas that don't interest you. After you have eliminated the easily discarded ideas you are ready to send the other opportunities through the rest of the selection process.

**Step 3: Examine the specific industry**. How easy is the business to enter and how much market growth should you expect? If the business is easy to enter and the market is a growing one, the business moves to the next level. Take for example a computer consulting company. Since you need very little investment to enter this market and the potential for growth is high, this business idea would move to the next level.

Don't drive yourself crazy trying to determine the answers to these questions. Use your gut feeling and your general impressions. If you are having trouble generating an opinion, you are probably not close enough to this business opportunity for it to be a serious consideration at this time. You now know if the businesses you are considering are right for you.

**Step 4: Answer two critical questions:** (1) Can I make enough money to make the venture worth my time? and, (2) How much competition is there? There is a quick calculation you can do to see if you can make money with your venture.

For example, you are considering baking and selling apple pies to people in your neighborhood. You are very interested in pie baking and have 20 years of pie baking experience. You can enter the market easily by using your home kitchen oven to prepare the pies. You feel the dessert market is growing based on the success of area bakeries and dessert shops.

But can you make enough money to justify your efforts? Calculate the number of pies you think you can sell. Be realistic about your oven capacity and your available time. Then determine how much you can charge. Subtract the cost of your ingredients, the cost of your time and other miscellaneous costs. Don't forget hidden costs such as extra energy from using your oven more. The amount left over is your payoff or economic return. Then decide if the return is worth your time.

Now consider your competition. Are there other pie bakers in your neighborhood with the same plan? Competition should not necessarily make you change your business plans, but you should find out if there is too much competition for the business venture to be worthwhile. Is the market flooded or saturated? Does your neighborhood have all the pie bakers it can handle? If the economic return is high and the competition is low or at least acceptable, the business opportunity moves to the next step.

**Step 5: Consider the general market environment.** What is the demand for the idea and is the timing right for this business? Be careful. Many times demand can be high while timing is poor. An example is the development of businesses in the healthcare industry during the mid 90s.

Although the demand for your healthcare product or service may be high, the uncertainty of the future of healthcare in general makes the timing of this business a potential concern. If the demand is high and the timing is good, the business passes and becomes one of the businesses that warrants further study.

Now you have a short list of business ideas that you believe can be successful. You will need to do more research on each idea to determine which one you will pursue first. You may uncover multiple ideas that you believe are good. You will probably want to start only one idea at a time, but the others should be saved for later use.

## Researching Your Top Ideas

Your local library will play an important part in your research. You will want to know as much as you can about each of your top business ideas. The research area of the library will have all the data that you care to read. Develop a relationship with the librarian in this section of the library.

He will be able to give you guidance on were to find the information you will need without wasting time.

Know what information you want. What information do you need to help you make an informed decision about your short list of business ideas? Some obvious questions are: Is the business area growing? Are their enough customers to support your business efforts? For example if your idea targets married, black, Jewish families with incomes under $100,000 a year, you will want to know how many people fit this description.

Keep in mind you are not building a watch. Don't spend too much time on a lot of grueling detail about the business itself. You are looking for data that will determine whether this is a good business area to enter. You will have plenty of time to learn more about the particular business processes.

I suggest you do your research in four hour spurts. Four hours is enough time to get into the data and not so long as to make the task torture. If you enjoy research, four hours may be too little time. Ask the librarian any questions that you may have. Go at your own pace. Keep your mind fresh. Take good notes on the sources of your information. You may want to revisit this data source again if you select this particular business idea. Do not spend more than twelve productive hours gathering information on businesses at this stage.

After doing your preliminary research on the top business opportunities, you will have all the information you need to decide on the business for you. If all of the ideas still look good, you will have to choose one and defer the other ideas for future ventures. Do not discard the data you have accumulated. You may want to start one of the other businesses at a later time. Most entrepreneurs have many researched business ideas waiting for the right time and team to implement them. Well-researched business ideas are valuable; keep all of yours.

7

# *Does Your Business Have to Be Unique?*

*"If you could pray for only one thing, let it be for an idea."*
— Percy Sutton
President & CEO
Inner City Broadcasting

*I*t is very rare that a business person will develop a business idea that will create an entirely new market. For example, if you had a pill that could be safely taken which guaranteed a person would maintain their ideal weight, you would have very little trouble getting people to buy it. There would be no competitors. You would have created a totally new market. Your marketing expenses would be low because all of the media services would see your product as being worthy of news reporting. Imagine being on the cover of top magazines and appearing on morning news and information programs.

Although African-Americans need to continue to stretch their imaginations in order to create new product innovations, a new market product is rare. If your product is not creating a new market, then your success depends on two strategies. You will either have to take some of the existing customers from your competition, or find a way to get a new set of customers to start using your product or service.

For example, imagine you want to start a new dry cleaning business in your neighborhood. You should assume that all the people wanting to get their clothes dry cleaned are getting the service performed by someone. If you are going to get customers for your new business, some other dry cleaning company will have to loose customers.

The only other way to grow your new business is to find a group of people who do not presently use any dry cleaning service. If your company has a service special enough to convince this new group to start using a dry cleaner, you will have expanded the market. An expanded market simply means that new people are now using the product or service.

Your business can expand the market with simple changes. Items such as location, ease of use, or a new use for an old product can all attract a new set of customers. The African-American community is often overlooked by large corporations. Making relatively minor changes to an established product may make it appealing to this overlooked population.

Expanding your market is a good strategy, but it is not mandatory. One of the two partners that we consulted with was very concerned about competition. While we were refining their business idea and completing the business plan, he continued to show us company after company that was doing the same thing these two wanted to do.

After he sent me four different articles on potential competitors, it was clear what he was trying to say. If someone else was doing what they wanted to do, he felt that the partners might have trouble succeeding with the venture. My opinion was quite the opposite: "Since competitors have seen this market as one lucrative enough for investment, then you must be on the right track." If the product or service had no potential, the other companies would have gone out of business. The evidence of a healthy amount of competition confirms your research that your idea is viable.

My response probably surprised him. **The real question is not, Is there competition?, but Do we have something that makes us different? What is our competitive advantage? Why should our prospective clients choose us?"** You must have answers to these questions. Unless you have that rare product I mentioned above, you will need a competitive advantage that allows you to take business from someone else.

The difference between you and your competition is your competitive advantage. Maintaining your advantage will require a benefit that is **sustainable.** A sustainable competitive advantage is an advantage one company has over its competition. The advantage is recognized by the customer and is difficult for the competition to replicate.

What should your sustainable competitive advantage be? Price is the most popular way for African Americans to separate our products from others. You simply scan your competition to see what they are charging and set your price below theirs. Although this the easiest way to set your product apart, it is also the easiest advantage to lose.

When the competition sees that you are taking their business because of your lower price, they need only lower their price as a response. These pricing actions could continue until one of you is out of business. Since you are the new company and probably have less money to last in a price war of this type, it will more than likely be you that is forced out of the market. Price is a good competitive weapon, but it is not a good sustainable competitive advantage.

A **competitive weapon is a short-term strategy.** A competitive weapon is good for gaining entry into a new market or dumping obsolete inventory. Do not be afraid to use price as a competitive weapon. Keep in mind that you must have something else to follow-up with that is more sustainable. Using a competitive weapon in place of a sustainable competitive advantage can be disastrous. The best sustainable competitive advantages revolve around internal processes that allow companies to deliver products more quickly, quarantee results or provide exceptional quality. Companies that can create a particular image or environment also have strong sustainable competitive advantages.

Look at your own purchase decisions for clues of sustainable competitive advantage. What would make you change your barber? Is there anything that would make you change where you get your car washed or where you shop for groceries? Are you a person focused on price? Does the combination of high quality and competitive price or value attract you? Maybe you are a prestige buyer, someone who cares about brand name and location.

For most of us our buying decisions depend on what item we are buying and how important it is to us. My wife only considers cost when it comes to groceries. In order toget her grocery business, you must provide double coupon offers, store brands and low prices. Yet, when she shops for clothes, she focuses on value. The price must be "acceptable," but the quality must be very good. To her the attractiveness of a college sweatshirt is its' thickness. If the sweatshirt is not thick enough, no price will be low enough to get her to buy.

**The key component to a sustainable competitive advantage is its perceived value by your customers.** A business that can establish **perceived value** or PV can sell anything. **Perceived value is created with the appropriate combination of image, quality, and price.** While attending a meeting of the Black Male Coalition, a volunteer group of black males in Cincinnati, one of the members noticed my Mont Blanc pen: "Not everyone carries a pen like that," he said.

His comment somehow made me feel important. The pen is a quality writing instrument. It looks nice, but so does a Cross pen. Why would a person spend $70 more for a Mont Blanc pen? The answer is PV. The Mont Blanc company has unlocked the secret  door to unlimited success. They have combined the right price with the correct image and top quality.

Perceived Value is **not** reserved for high-priced and high-quality image products. McDonald's fast food restaurant has also caged the power of PV. They have used a standard system to give customers a consistent experience. When you pull from the highway into a McDonald's restaurant you know exactly what to expect: clean restrooms, Big Macs, and a drive thru window. McDonald's customers perceive this consistency as having value.

Determining your own buying beliefs will help you make your product fit your mentality. If you are a prestige buyer, then a discount  shop may not be right for you. There are no set rules. You must consider your competition, your target market, and your available marketing funds.

*8*

# Pricing the Product

*"No one can figure out your worth but you."*
—Pearl Bailey
Singer & Actress

*T* he proper pricing of your product or service is critical to the success of your business. By pricing your product or service correctly, you give yourself a better opportunity to sell your product and make a profit. It is a good idea to figure your product or service price using two methods: cost basis and market basis.

**Cost basis** pricing is **the totaling of all the costs involved in providing a product or service and adding your profit amount.** Including **all** the costs is important. Do not forget the hidden items such as the cost of your time or the time of volunteer family members. Why is the inclusion of these costs so important? Unless you and your family plan to continue to work for free, you need to include this cost.

**Cost basis pricing will help you to determine if you can produce the product or perform the service at a price that can be sold in the marketplace.** Many African-American business owners ignore costs for services that they may receive free of charge during the early stages of their business. Getting help from other people is good. It can help get your business off to a strong start, but free help is not a long-term solution and therefore should have no bearing on the price of your product.

A friend of mine started a soul-food restaurant. We will call him Sam. Sam figured his cost based on the obvious expenditures: rent, food, plates, licenses, beverages, etc. He figured that his wife, teen-age daughter, and himself would provide the personnel needed to run the restaurant. After two months of constant work at the restaurant, Sam's family help began to give way. His daughter became busy with school activities, and his wife needed to spend more time at home with their younger child. This left Sam in need of workers, so he hired two reliable employees.

Although the new help was good, Sam could not afford to sell his food at the previous prices and still make a profit. Sam was getting plenty of customers but was not making any money. The problem was that he had not figured the cost of needed personnel in to the price of the meals. He thought his family would be there forever.

Add all the costs in at the beginning. Be realistic! If you can get some of your expense items for less or no cost at all, then your business will have larger profits. But do not depend on freebees.

Taking into account the costs that it takes to produce or provide your product is only one way of setting the price you charge your customer for the product. **Market basis pricing** is the second method. Market basis is **the price that someone is willing to pay for your product.** One way to figure market price for a product or service is to price it according to what your target market is willing to pay. That price insures that your customers will be happy with the price and that you will maximize your product's profit potential.

Another way to figure the market price for a product or service is to determine the worth of the product to the customer. What will be the impact to the customer. Will it help them save money? How much? Will it save them time? How much is that time worth? Determining your product price using the market basis can be tricky. Simply stated, you must find out how much people are paying for your product or service. Research products that are positioned in the same market as your product. If your product is high-quality and high-price, you should find out the price of other high-quality and high-price competitors.

InfraStructure faced a pricing dilemma during the startup of a marketing consulting division. My partner and I had developed a new service where we would consult with other engineering companies on effective sales and marketing techniques. We knew our potential clients had all made investments in hiring full-time marketing personnel. All of their efforts in marketing had failed. The question was how much would it be worth to them to save their new marketing person time and improve their effectiveness?

We estimated we could save the marketing person half of their marketing time, so we set the price for our service at roughly half of the individual's salary. My partner thought the price was too high, and so did the customer. We then showed the benefits of our service. We translated the benefits into time and money. Once they saw how much money they could save, they were sold, and price was no longer an issue. We had moved the issue from price to value.

The only question left was whether they thought we could deliver on our promises. If the answer to this question was no, then a lower price still would not have won the business. The process of pricing your product is rarely this easy, but setting the price based on the value of your product can be done.

It is often a good idea to compare the cost basis price to the market basis price. You will not be able to sell a product for more than the market basis price. So if the cost basis price is higher than the market basis price, you should either find a way to lower your cost or abandon this particualar product.

## How Much Are You Worth: Setting the Price for Professional Services

My research for this book shows that African-American businesses are often formed based on the professional skills of the founder and business owner. Service businesses that offer assistance with accounting, public relations, speech writing, computer programming, and business consulting are all examples of professional service firms. Blacks frequently start professional services companies because of the low cost of start up. It is very easy to mis-price your professional services, so I have included this section to give you a better idea of how to price a professional service business for long-term stability.

Pricing your professional services can be tricky. Your objective should be to charge what people will pay for your level of talent while building a business you can sustain over a long term. Consider looking at your pricing strategy in two ways. First, look at your pricing based on external factors. Evaluate your personal skill and talents. What skills do you have? How experienced are you? Look at your environment. What are your customers willing to pay? Does your geographic location impact what you can charge? You should also consider others in your business. Do you have any competition? What do they charge? The last external factor is your level of need. How badly do you need the work or the client? The entire evaluation of external factors is called the

YEON system. YEON stands for You, the Environment, Others in the business, and your Need.

Now that you are aware of the external issues affecting the price of your professional service, you will want to consider the internal issues involved. You need to determine the amount of money you desire to earn. The easiest way to figure this number is to add up all of your real business expenses and your salary needs and divide by the number of hours you expect to bill. Your real expenses include insurance, taxes, retirement contributions, office rent, supplies, and telephone and marketing costs. As always, it is important to be sure to include all of your costs. Include costs that you don't have now but will have as your business grows. You don't want to have to increase your billing rates because your business begins to grow.

If you have trouble getting all the numbers you need for this calculation, there is a dependable short cut. Simply add between 25% and 33% to what you want to earn to cover your expenses. This will give you a good estimate of how much revenue your professional services business must bring in. You then divide by the number of hours you expect to bill to get your hourly rate. For example, you wish to earn $45,000 a year. Add $13,500 (30%) for expenses. This means your annual revenue will have to be $58,500.

Calculate the number of hours you plan to bill. There are an average of 20 working days in each month. When you subtract holidays, vacation time and time you will spend marketing, you are left with 200 days or 1600 hours of billing time per year. Your hourly billing rate would be your required annual revenue divided by the total billable hours for the year. Continuing our example from above, divide $58,500 by 1600 hours for a result of $37 an hour. Saying you have 200 days of time available to bill does not mean you will bill all of this time. Be prepared to grow your business to this point. If you wish to work less and still make the same money, then you will have to raise your hourly rate.

**Figure 8.1. Calculating Your Hourly Rate for Professional Services**

| Example | | Your Rate |
|---|---|---|
| $45,000 | Desired Earnings | $_____ |
| $13,500+ | Business Expenses | $_____ |
| -------------- | | |
| $58,500 | Revenue | $_____ |
| -1600 | Hours of Billing Time | - _____ |
| $37/hr | Hourly Rate | $_____/Hr. |

Always consider your long-term goals when you are setting your price. Remember the external issues affecting your price, but do not let them dictate your rate completely. If you lower your rates because you really need the work, it will be difficult to charge that client any other price. You may be stuck charging a lower price forever, and this will impact your ability to stay in business over time. African-American business owners often feel they need the work too badly. We are willing to take less than we are worth in order to get our businesses started or to get an opportunity in a large corporation. Be careful. Make it clear that you have lowered your prices for the opportunity to show your skills.

When you quote a price your potential client thinks is too high, reduce the scope of the project not your price. Changing the price implies that you were charging too much in the first place. If the client cannot afford you to perform all of the work, offer to do a portion of the work and to provide advice on the rest of the project. Less scope will mean a lower total bill, but you will not have to change your hourly rate. The client will value your respect for your own skills and your credibility will rise in their eyes. If your services are priced correctly, the client will not be able to find someone else with your skills to do the job for any less.

Really take the time to develop your pricing. Examine both the cost and market basis strategies. Consider all the costs you have now and all costs that you expect to incur in the future. The right pricing means profits; the wrong pricing could mean disaster.

# Part III:
# Who Will You Sell It to, and How Will You Sell It to Them?

**Knowing your customer** is a necessity. What you will need to know will depend on many things. The key is to have a **focused set of customers**. Customers who can and will buy your product are the ones you will want to gather needed information about. **Your customer group should be large enough to ensure diversity but not so large that there are too many customers for your business to handle.** Once you decide who you will sell your product or service to, you will have to decide how you are going to sell it to them.

There are many effective ways to market your product. Mass mailing, telemarketing, and direct sales calls are all effective methods. The method you choose will be determined by your market, product or service, time, and budget. With a little planning and creativity, you can effectively market with little money.

Make sure you understand the various marketing methods, and plan your strategy early. The following sections will provide you with the background information that you will need in order to get to know your customers and plan your marketing strategy accordingly.

9

# Focusing on the Customer

*"The key is knowing your customer, not just marching in and offering an objectively attractive deal."*

—Harvey Mackay
Author

## What Should You Know about the Customer?

*W*ho are the people that need or want your product or service? This is the first question to answer when developing an effective marketing plan. The people, agencies and companies who want your product or service are your target market. Your target market is the group about whom you will want to collect detailed information. Review your product to decide what information you will need.

Gravely & Associates, the business education and development company that I founded, struggled with this concept as we developed our marketing plan. The company mission was to educate and develop small businesses and their personnel.

Our target market was small business. As we analyzed our market environment, we realized there was a great deal of competition. There were many companies in the marketplace with small businesses as a target market. We also realized that our target market had its' own barriers to using our product. The small business market often could not afford to pay the price for our quality education, training, and consulting. We had to find a different way to serve our potential clients.

We looked for other agencies that supported our target market, such as the Urban League, community development corporations, business incubators, and professional associations. These groups often have budgets to perform training or are willing to write grants to get funding for innovative programs that will further the mission of their agency. We had to include these groups in our marketing plan.

Knowing information about your target market will help you form your marketing strategy. **Knowing your customer means understanding their needs, issues, and barriers.**

The first step to understanding your customers is to identify the buying market for your product or service. **Buying markets are broken into two major categories: consumer products and business-to-business product markets.** Consumer products are those products purchased by individuals for their personal use or enjoyment.

Examples of consumer products are toothpaste, clothes, home cleaning services, and single family washing machines. Business-to-business products or services are those that are sold to a business for use in the activities of their business. Products such as copier paper, office cleaning services, and computer programming services are considered business-to-business products. Some products fit in both categories.

Knowing the **type of business** you are in will help you know what data is important. What information do you need to tell you if a person or business will want to buy your product or service? Figure 9.1 gives you some examples of

**Figure 9.1. Examples of What You Need to Know About Your Customer**

---

## Examples of What You Need To Know

**For  A Consumer Product or Service**
  Age of consumer
  Income level
  Geographic location
  Marital Status
  Shop by mail?

**Business to Business (or Government**
  Computer systems? Type & Amount
  Sales force size
  Number of locations
  Shipping activity
  Certification needed
  Contact department (Contact person if possible)
  Procurement process
  Minority Business Enterprise programs

---

typical items you may need to know about your target market based on the category of your product.

Use this list as a guide, but marketing your product or service will require you to obtain more detailed and specific data. Paint the picture of the perfect customer for your business. What is it about that customer that makes them perfect? These are the characteristics you should be looking for. Find the target market and determine the information you will need to sell to them effectively.

## Making Your Ex-boss Your Customer

If your business is providing the same product or service

you performed as an employee of another company, consider making that company your client. Many African-American businesses have gotten their start by making their ex-boss their first customer. Noncompetitive business services or project-oriented consulting are the easiest areas to form a new vendor-client relationship.

A personal computer professional in a small midwest town performed a very specialized computer software job for a large steel company. Feeling frustrated with the company bureaucracy, he decided to leave the company and make his ex-employer his first customer. This new structure gave the new business owner his freedom and the large company got a knowledgeable computer consultant. If the idea of making your previous employer your customer appeals to you, keep these four thoughts in mind.

First, **make sure your personal services or products are desired by your employer.** If the employer does not value you as an employee, they will probably not want to do business with you as an entrepreneur. This is a tough question to ask yourself, but it is best to be honest with yourself now than to find out your true value after you have quit your job and started your business.

Second, **get a feel for the possibility of your employer doing business with you as an independent business owner.** Is your employer one that would be upset if you left to start a non-competing business? Some employers welcome this move toward independence; others see it as disloyalty or a condemnation of the corporate environment.

Third, as you move from employee to vendor, **consider the value of your relationships.** Your biggest challenge will be maintaining the inside relationships that you have developed. Many of those who were co-workers will become customers. Some will encourage you while others may be jealous. Yesterday you were a peer. Today you are a business owner who wants business. Never take your relationships for granted. Maintain your contacts and be professional.

Finally, **have a plan before you leave the stability of your current job.** Although you'll have the commitment from your employer to become your first customer, you need to plan much like other start-up businesses. Some start ups see their new corporate customer as a long-term "sugar daddy" who is willing to do an ever increasing amount of business with their small business.

Although establishing relationships with large corporate partners is a great start-up strategy, reliance on them for survival is a prescription for going out-of-business. The failed business garbage can is full of trashed African American businesses that relied on one major customer. Use your commitment with your ex-boss as a starting point and then spend between 60% and 70% of your time finding new clients. Be prepared to really go it on your own.

## Monitoring Your Customer Mix

**Customer mix** is a term used to describe the makeup of your clients as a group. **Customer makeup is the distribution of the type and the number of customers you have.** African-American businesses notoriously have either too many or too few customers. For example, we often form alliances with large companies to provide products or services. So satisfied with this single large customer, we fail to continue working to get a good mix of other customers.

A few years back, I read of a situation where a large company had formed a twenty year contract with a minority company to supply all of the cleaning products for the company's locations. When the contract was signed the minority company's customer mix was just a few customers.

This new large customer was responsible for nearly 100%

of the minority business' revenue. The customer then had all the power. They could pay when they wanted. They could demand the price they wanted. The large company was in complete control of the minority business. This is an example of position you do not want to be in for long. All of the benefits were with the large company. This minority company failed to take this opportunity to grow and diversify it's customer base.

This may seem like an extreme case to you but many black businesses are held captive by a majority company. Any customer accounting for more than 30% of your company revenue could control your company. Diversify your customers and constantly monitor the mix. Periodically ask yourself this question: Can I afford to lose any one of my customers and stay in business? Take the time to do the math. Subtract the revenue of any particular customer and recalculate your income statements and evaluate the results.

I am not saying it is bad to do business with large companies. Of course, you want to enter in to good, solid contracts with as many customers as you can. But you must be careful not to put any one customer in a position to control the terms of your company. You must be able to say no to a customer and still survive. Blacks need to put more focus on long-term businesses. We cannot expect to develop long-term businesses if the customer is "dictating" the terms of the deal. You started your business to be independent. Do not let some other company own yours.

Keeping the right customer mix is very difficult. Although I warn against having too few customers, having too many can also be a problem. **Picking up new customers at any cost is never good.** Customers that do not pay on time or want prices too low for you to make money, are customers your business does not need. The 80-20 rule says that 20% of your customer typically provide 80% of your profits (Figure 9.2).

The other 80% of your customers are using your resources, taking up your time, and adding very little to your profits.

Find these poor customers and give them to your competition. **All business is not good business.** Selling one computer at a profit is better than selling 100 computers and losing a dollar on each one. **Find and keep the customers who truly value your product or service.** You want to find

**Figure 9.2. The 80/20 Rule: 20% of Your Customers Will Produce 80% of Your Profits**

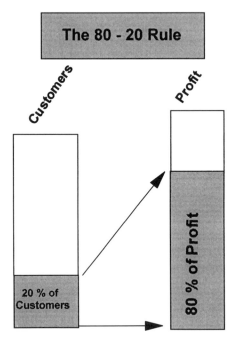

situations were you and the customer both win. These are the relationships that last and will make your business successful.

Defining your customers takes time and a willingness to understand their desires. **Knowing the customer is the beginning of your entire marketing plan.** Not knowing who your customers are will waste your time and resources. You cannot sell effectively sell to a group that you do not know.

*10*
_____

# *Effective Marketing Methods*

*"You never know which key unlocks the safe."*
—Bryant Gumbel,
The Today Show

*Y* ou now know your target market. You have researched your market to determine the attributes that will help you sell your product or service. Use this information to formulate your marketing strategy. The data you collected about your target market will dictate the type of marketing strategies that you use. Few companies use only one type of marketing strategy. Most put together a mix of methods directed at the buying habits of their potential clients and the type of product being marketed.

## *Marketing Through the Mail—Mass Mailing*

Mass mailing can be a very effective and low cost way to market to your potential customers. **Mass mailing is the mailing of "scientifically" developed material aimed at motivating individuals to take some positive action to the benefit of your product.** By manipulating the few variables involved in mass mailing, you can control the results of your mail marketing efforts.

The first variable to consider is the quality of your mailing list. There are companies in the business of building, maintaining and selling mailing list to business people like you. Make sure you are dealing with a reputable mailing list company. Ask questions about how they get their list and how often and by what methods the lists are updated.

Quality mailing list companies will be used to these questions and will be glad to give you answers. Many legitimate firms will ask to see a sample of the mailer you wish to send. They want to be sure your firm is real, and you are not planning to market illegal products through the mail. Shop multiple list companies and compare the price and professionalism of each firm. A good list can give you a variety of information. You can get lists based on zip code, area code, age, number of children, marital status, gender, credit cards, smokers, veterans, and occupation to name just a few.

This method of marketing is designed for businesses that want to mail a large number of pieces. The biggest mistake of first time mass mailers is sending out too few mailing pieces and expecting too high of a response. Dr. Timothy S. Hillebrand, president of Synergetics International, Moscow, ID, and a mass mailing expert, feels that if your list is not at least 5,000 names large, you should purchase the list with telephone numbers and consider using the telephone to contact your potential customers.

The percentage of customer response to a mass mailing is very low. A one percent return is considered good, and anything higher is outstanding. So if you have a list with 5,000 people on it, you should expect no more than 50 responses. A list quantity of 5,000 or larger is a rule of thumb but not a hardfast rule. We have sent mail advertising in quantities as small as 60 pieces. We targeted the market very carefully, and the campaign was repeated often.

After five different mailings and a year and a half, we got two new customers. In our case, each customer was worth enough business to make our small mailings worth our effort. You must make sure a 1% return of whatever number you choose to send is worth the expense of the mailing. Low returns to your mail marketing will be difficult to get used to, but 1% is all you should expect.

Another common mistake of new mass mailers is trying to make the mailing look personal. Handwritten envelopes are a clear indicator your company is small potatoes. The big mass mailing companies would never handwrite the envelope. Use labels or type the address directly on the envelopes. Use a computer (see Chapter 27 on using technology to gain advantage) to create and maintain your mailing list. This method will save you time, money and improve your image.

The same thing goes for using bulk mail. Some people believe your mailer will be more readily received if it is sent using first class mail. Professional mass mailing companies always use bulk rate mail for their marketing. If your mailing is large enough, use bulk mail. The bulk rate will save you money and will make your mailing more professional.

With your mailing list complete and your expectations for success realistic, you are ready to prepare your mailing pieces. Mailing pieces are the contents of your mass mailing. These pieces can include cover letters, brochures, postcards, and anything else you think will persuade your potential client to do business with your company. What goes into your mailing will depend on your budget and the buying habits of your target market.

You can use the techniques of the professionals to make your mailing pieces more effective. Start saving the mass mailings you receive. Consider what attracts your attention to certain types of mailings. Look at the words the marketer uses to get their point across. You will notice that many of the mass mailing pieces you receive use the same words to grab your attention. This is not by accident.

Remember the following basics as you prepare your mailing pieces:

**1) Make your pieces easy to read and understand.** Test your mailings on someone who knows nothing about what you are doing. Be sure the person can easily understand your product's features and benefits. Your instructions for buying should be easy to find and to perform.

**2) State benefits boldly and often.** Explain clearly what it is you are selling and why the recipient must have your product. Appeal to the needs of your customer. Stress how your product will change the buyer's life for the better. Key words in a mass mailing document are you, advantage, benefit, love, easy, and new and improved.

**3) Choose your colors carefully.** Color is as important as the words on your mailing pieces. Use colors like royal blue, green and black. Be careful about using red. Red means negative or debt to many people, so use red sparingly. Green means go or money. Royal blue means power and indicates a solid business. Black is stable and can be used any time you are in doubt. It would be a good idea to look at the mailings you get again. What colors are they using and how does their approach make you feel? Copy the colors and styles you like.

**4) Make it easy for the customer to respond to your request.** People who respond to mass mailing campaigns often do so as an impulse. They receive the mailer, like what they see, and make the decision to buy right then. Your pieces must cater to this impulse by making the ordering process simple, painless, and quick. If the customer must order by mail, make the order form simple and quick. If possible include a postage paid envelope for convenience. If the response can be by telephone, consider a 1-800 number to make the call easy and inexpensive for the buyer. Make sure you have setup a 24 hour answering system which allows the customer to call when the feeling hits. There are many companies who offer answering services with 1-800 numbers as a package. Call different answering service companies to determine the cost for this type of service.

Even before you design your mailing pieces, you want to keep three things utmost in your mind when considering a mass mailing campaign: (1) getting a good and reliable list, (2) making sure the marketing pieces are well-planned and professional, (3) repeating your mailing multiple times. Sending the mailer many times is especially important for new products or new companies. It will take two or more mailings to get your market used to seeing your company name.

Consider sending low cost flyers or postcards first. Then change your pieces the next time. You want to make the pieces different enough to notice, but not so different you cannot tell that they are from the same company. Mass mailing takes patience. It will be difficult to tell if mailing campaigns have been successful. Surveying clients will help you to determine if your marketing efforts have been paying off.

## Marketing Over the Telephone— Telemarketing

Telemarketing can be a very effective tool when you are trying to market your product or service. **Telemarketing is selling your product or services over the telephone.** This method of marketing is very similar to the mass mailing approach mentioned above. **Telemarketing is an exceptional strategy to use for lists that you feel are too short for an effective mass mailing.** Just as in mass mailing, it is important that you understand your market and know your objectives. Who are the people you want to reach and what do you want them to do?

**The first step in developing an effective telemarketing program is to get a good calling list.** The questions should be the same as with the mass mailing approach. Your telemarketing campaign will be a waste if you don't spend the time to get the right list. You must be sure you are calling the people who want and can afford to buy your product or service.

Next you must create a telemarketing **script, a pre-written conversation that is meant to introduce your idea to the prospect on the telephone.** The script should be brief, businesslike, and friendly. It should clearly state who you are, why you are calling, and what you want. To increase your success rate, anticipate any objections the prospect may have. Then prepare responses to these objections ahead of time.

Having this objection handling script prepared will make you more confident making the calls. You will have just a few seconds to win a customer on the telephone, so your pitch must be good, concise and smooth.

Practice the script enough so that it does not sound like you are reading. Really try to have a conversation with the prospect. Say your name and the name of your company slowly. Tell the prospect the two of you have never met. This will stop the prospect from trying to place your voice. You want them processing the information you are giving not trying to figure out who they are speaking to. Listen to their objections and use your prepared responses to turn objections into opportunities.

You are probably thinking you do not want to use this marketing method because you hate getting telemarketing calls yourself. There is no way for me to convince you to like telemarketing. The only thing I can say is that telemarketing works. Everyone hates getting the calls, but telemarketing gets people to buy. Your biggest challenge will be overcoming your own fear of calling people that you do not know. Remember they do not know you either. The worst they can say is no. Trust me, it doesn't hurt. Hang-up the telephone and call the next name. This form of marketing is one of the most cost effective of any marketing method. If you do not have much money, you should get to the telephone and start calling.

## Direct Sales Calls—Getting Your Foot in the Door

When you are making a direct sales call, it is important to meet with the person that can say yes or no to your product or service. If the decision is being made by committee or a bid process, it is still a good idea to meet with as many committee members as possible. If the selection is made using the bid process, you will want all the information you can get so your bid reflects the top priorities of the customer. If the selection is made by committee, the more committee members you know the better your chances of succeeding.

Our firm learned this lesson the hard way. When our engineering company was still fairly new, we went after a large project in Cleveland, Ohio. We knew the competition was going to be tough, so we spent considerable time putting together our response to the city's bid request. Our proposal was top quality, complete, and accurate.

After about thirty days, I called the project owner to follow-up on the status of the project. The project manager, whom I had never met, told me our firm was not selected. In an effort to improve our responses to bids, I asked why he felt we were not selected. His response was "No one on the selection committee knew your firm." He went on to say

"Our schedule was tight on this project, and no one wanted to take a chance on someone we didn't know." It was a lesson well learned. Never believe a simple response to a request for a proposal will win you the business.

You need to know the person or people making the decision, and they must want you to win. If the right person wants you to win, few issues can make you lose. It will take more time and effort for African-Americans to build these relationships. But there are more and more blacks in key positions who can make decisions in our favor, and these relationships can be built.

You will need a plan of attack and the will to get to the people you need to know. How do you get the chance to meet with the decision maker at your prospective customer? It is often as simple as calling them on the telephone and asking for a meeting. If you know who the decision maker is, calling them is the best method. If you do not know who to call, call the general office number and ask for the name of the person who controls the purchase of the product or service in which you are most interested.

Get the name and telephone number and start calling. Be sure you know how to spell and pronounce the person's name. Our firm was pursuing a contract with a particular customer for more than a year. The key contact's name was John Kniepper (the k is pronounced). His secretaries would determine who knew and could speak to John based on who pronounced his name correctly. If you pronounced his name incorrectly, they assumed you did not know John and they would take a message. If you pronounced the name correctly, you would be sent through to Mr. Kniepper's line.

When you make your call, be prepared to talk to a secretary whose job is to screen people trying to market their products. Do not take it personally. Be polite but direct. Explain why you are calling and what you want. If the person you wish to speak to is not available, leave a message. The message should include your name, the name of your company, and your telephone number. Wait two or three days for a return call and then call again. It is you who wants this meeting not the person you are calling.

You may have to be persistent to get to some people. Most purchasing agents, executives, and decision makers get many calls just like yours each day. Polite persistence will separate you from the crowd. If you continue to have trouble reaching the person, try a different contact media. Send your prospect a short letter (Figure 10.1) explaining your company and your desire to meet them in person. Continue to alternate your contact styles until you get the opportunity to speak directly with the decision maker.

When you speak to the person you need to be ready to tell them why they should agree to meet with you. How will it benefit them? Once I tried to contact a potential client for almost three months. He was the architect for a major university in our area. My calls were so frequent the secretary knew my voice and my number by heart. The prospect never returned my calls. Finally, I caught the client in his office.

After pursuing him for over a month, I had just a few minutes to convince him to meet with me in person. He needed to hear a little about our company and the potential benefits that we could provide to the university. The prospect was very polite and agreed to a meeting. The meeting turned into great business for our company and the client is now one of our best references. He still does not return my calls. I don't take it personally because I know that is the way this client operates.

Getting your foot in the door is easier if you believe that it must happen. If your prospect is reluctant to meet with you, ask for 11 minutes of her time. Offer to give $100 to her favorite charity if you run over the allotted time without her

**Figure 10.1. Sample Introduction Letter**

July 6, 1993

Linda Jones
Director of Quality
City of Elms
166 City St.
Elms, Ohio 44448

Dear Ms. Jones:

  4-Word Company is a professional business consulting firm. We specialize in company structure improvement projects in northeastern Ohio. We are a minority owned company located in Elms.
  Our company is certified with the State as a professional consultant, pre-qualified with the National Board to provide business consulting services. I have included a brief flyer on the types of services 4-Word can provide. We would like to work with you to get involved in quality improvement projects in our city.
  I will call in the next few days to arrange a meeting to discuss our qualifications further. Thank you in advance for your assistance.

                                        Sincerely,


                                        Paul J. Smith
                                        Partner

permission. Your creativity will be appreciated, and you will probably get your meeting. Even if you use an ingenious approach, you will not get in to see all of the people you want to. Some people will not want to meet with you, but Some prospects will be worth more effort. Give it a real try over a period of time. Consider what you have to gain when you get through. Pick up the telephone and place the call.

## Direct Sales Calls—Being Effective in the Call

One of the few common threads running through all of business is the need to make an effective sales call. At some time in your career, you have undoubtedly had to sell someone on you, your company, or both. Think back to your last job interview. You presented yourself on paper through your resume. You continued to pursue the job by answering and asking key questions during the interview. Job interviewing is very similar to a sales call. The objectives are the same. You want the interviewer to pick you. You want to win his attention, respect, and confidence.

**Many good business ideas have failed because the business owner failed to see the value of selling.** Most business people have problems with selling because of their fear of **"engaging"** the customer. Since most small business owners do not have sales experience, they feel uncomfortable asking prospects for business. Just as an interview is the doorway to a job, selling is the doorway to lucrative contracts. The following tips were developed to help individuals with little or no sales experience make more effective sales calls:

**1) Be yourself.** Try thinking of a sales call as a conversation about how the benefits of your business will fill the needs of your prospect. We all have a basic ability to hold conversations. Don't change your personal style (unless it is offensive) because you are trying to get someone to do business with you. If you feel nervous, it may be a good idea to say so: *"Ms. Client, I don't do much of this marketing stuff ,so if I appear a little nervous please excuse me."* Be sincere and you will gain the respect of your potential customer.

A marketing representative called on my partner and I a few months ago. His company sold engineering related equipment and services. He was following up on a lead that he had received about our needing an engineering plotter, a large printer common in the engineering companies.

As the marketing representative began to ask us questions about our company, we both noticed that he had a serious speech impediment. At first it was difficult to understand him, but after a short time we were involved in an active conversation. The representative was being himself. He was confident in his product's ability to help our business. His manner of delivery was not important. He was knowledgeable, responsive and earned our respect as a professional. We asked him to put together an actual proposal.

He returned the information on the date he promised, and we bought the equipment a month later. Whatever you do, be yourself. You will be more comfortable and your customer will be ready to hear what you have to say.

**2) Prepare ahead of time.** Plan for your sales call in advance. Know something about your prospect and their organization. Understand where and why your product or service may be viewed as a benefit. The way your product or service will be used will depend on the particular needs of your prospect.

Find out how your product can be used by the prospective client. Can your business help the client during peak times? Will your business be able to perform tasks on an as needed basis without the client going through the expense of adding permanent staff? Do your homework on the client. Are they in the process of downsizing or outsourcing?

Think about how your business may fit before you make the call. You should also know what you want from the sales call. Do you expect an order? Further information? A bid request? Always have the objective of the call clear in your mind.

**3) Build rapport.** When you arrive on time (not early or late) for the meeting, thank the prospect for seeing you. Look for items hanging on the wall or sitting on the desk or book shelf for clues of the client's interests. Ask them an open-ended question about themselves or their company. An open-ended question is one that cannot be answered by a single word. Questions that start with how, where, or describe will almost surely be open-ended. Open-ended questions will get the prospect talking, and they will feel that you are interested in listening to them and their concerns.

Once a person begins openly talking, it is easier to keep them talking. Be sure that your inquires are sincere. Statements like "Oh what beautiful children" may be a little too much. Only ask questions you are interested in knowing the answers to. Ask the question and listen intently to the answer, but concentrate on steering the conversation back to business.

After a brief conversation, look for ways to direct the focus of your meeting to business. Sometimes you can make a smooth transition, and other times it will not be as smooth. If the chit chat is going too long, consider using the following transitional statement. While looking at your watch, say "Oh my goodness time is slipping away, and I want to be sure not to over stay my welcome. The reason for our meeting today is to ......". Using this statement will show that you care about your prospect's time and that you are ready to move on to business.

**4) Generate interest.** Make a simple statement about why you are there and what your company provides. Mention the benefits to the client in your interest building statement. An example of an interest building statement is:

*Mr. Customer, the reason I asked to meet with you today is to introduce you to our company. We are a computer technology company. We are in the business of helping our clients reduce the amount of money they spend on computer systems. I wanted to talk with you about the op-*

*portunity of providing these benefits to your organization.*
*How do you select your computer technology consultants?*

This approach will lead into conversation about the prospect's needs and their selection process. Knowledge of what the prospect needs and how they make purchase selections is the core information that you will need in order to get them to do business with you. In addition to gaining useful information from the client, you will also give the prospective client an opportunity to pose any questions they have about your company.

**5) Listen! Listen! Listen!** Some sales people believe they have to tell all they know about their company and product in the first sales call. Quite the opposite is true. By asking opened ended questions and listening closely to the answers, you can find out what is important to the prospect. You'll know how she makes decisions and what projects may be coming soon.

You can uncover how your company could be of benefit to the prospect. You must be prepared to really listen. Listening is not thinking about what you are going to say next while the prospect is answering your last question. Listening is actively hearing and processing information for understanding.

**6) Tie needs to benefits.** After listening to the prospect's needs you are ready to tell him how you can specifically help with his situation. Using the words of the prospect, tell him how your product or service will be a perfect solution for his problem. It is important to use the prospect's words. If they used the term return on investment to describe how they make decisions, then you should speak to how your product will maximize return on investment.

If the prospect mentioned that his company wanted to cut costs by 15%, then tell your potential client how your product or service can assist them in achieving that specific goal. Using the clients words will make sure your message is understood. Mentioning the clients specific words will let the customer know you have been listening and you understand his business needs. An example benefit statement is: *"Mr. Customer you mentioned a need to lower your overall building maintenance cost. By using our preferred maintenance offering, you may be able to lower your building cleaning cost by as much as 15%."*

**7) Close the business.** You know what the client needs. You know how your product or service can help the prospect meet their objectives. You were prepared. You listened and you have earned the right to ask for what you want. If there are no other outstanding issues, then ask for the business. If you think your next step should be a formal proposal, then suggest a formal proposal as the next step. Whatever your meeting objective was, ask for it at the time of the meeting. This is the moment that makes us all uneasy. To make it easier, remember the prospect knows why you are there.

If you are really nervous about asking for the business, practice your closing statement before you get to the sales call. Your statement should be brief and direct. Do not leave any room for the client to misunderstand what you are asking. An example of a good closing statement is:

*"Ms. Customer I have shown you how our company can help you improve the quality of your cleaning while reducing your maintenance cost by 15%. When can we begin cleaning your facility so you can begin to get the benefits we have discussed?"*

If the client has objections to what you have suggested, use the objection handling technique outlined in the next section.

**8) Review and exit.** You are close to the end of a very successful sales call. Review the items that each of you agreed upon during the meeting. Make sure you have written down any action items. Action items are tasks that must be completed. These tasks should always have dates assigned to them. Simply saying you will do something means nothing. Giving the task a date will make it real and important. Never leave the next client contact entirely in the hands of the prospect. When the prospect tells you they will call you next, ask them when. Let them know you will call them if you do not hear from them in the stated period of time. Be polite but very businesslike. Do not give control to the prospect. You want to always leave the door open for further conversation.

Making an effective sales call is possible for anyone. As with most skills, practice will help you feel more comfortable and confident making calls. For most businesses, making quality sales calls is imperative for your success. Sales calls build relationships and relationships mean business. Make the time to make sales calls.

## Objection Handling—What If They Say "NO?"

We have reviewed the key techniques required to make a successful sales call. But no matter how well your sales call goes, the customer will probably have some question or objection to what you are trying to sell. The first thing to do when you think the customer has raised an objection is to listen closely. Pay attention to all the customer wants to tell you. You want to be sure you that have heard all of the concerns the customer may have.

Once you feel the customer is done stating the objection or objections, restate the objection in your own words to be sure you have a clear understanding. The worst thing you can do is misunderstand the objection and respond incorrectly. An example of how you may clarify the objection is "Just to be sure that I understand, Ms. Customer, are you saying you are concerned about that our service may conflict with your business operation?"

Now you clearly understand the customer's concern, and you are ready to go on. Before you respond, you should empathize with the customer. Empathizing with the customer shows that you understand their concern. You want them to feel that their objection is ok and welcome. The sentence I use is "I see your concern exactly. I had a customer just the other day with the same concern." This will put the customer at ease and may actually help them feel like they are being more cautious buyers. With this step, you are already starting to build their confidence in their decision to buy. Each objection by a customer is another chance for you to again sell them on the benefits of your business.

The most important step in the objection handling process is to turn the objection into a benefit of your product or service. This may seem difficult to do but will become second nature with practice. Every issue has at least two sides.

You must be confident enough in your product to be ready to present the positive to any negative that may arise. An example of a benefit statement follows from the empathy statement used before is:

> _"I see your concern exactly. I had a customer just the other day with the same concern. What they found was that our service actually helped the efficiency of their business."_

You want to go on to explain how this benefit happened.

The last step of objection handling is making sure that you have answered the objection and that the customer is satisfied. Simply ask the customer "Have I answered that concern? Do you have any other questions?". Once the customer is ready, move on to the end of your sales call.

## Marketing Your Business with Little Money

The previous sections have reviewed basic marketing strategies. Now that you know what marketing methods are available, let us look at what strategies are realistic for you based on the money that you have to spend. Many minority businesses toil unsuccessfully in the fields for years because of a lack of expertise or money for marketing. Managing a successful small business involves the continued balancing of limited resources. My partner and I always caution our associates to keep close tabs on their use of time and money. Time and money are the primary assets of a small business, and this is especially true in the area of marketing.

Many minority business owners often ask me "How can I market my business with no money?" Keeping your marketing costs under control is very important. Every dollar you spend on marketing is a dollar less in profit for the business. No one believes in the importance of marketing more than I do, but your marketing costs must be managed. If your marketing budget is small or even nonexistent, there are still some things that you can do to market your business effectively.

The key to marketing on a tight budget is not to waste any time or money. Before you invest any time or money in a marketing program, know what you want as an outcome and know what it takes to get your customers to buy. By knowing these two things, you will lower your chances of wasting your limited resources. The following are examples of marketing programs that will help you market your business effectively with little or no money:

**1) Do the marketing yourself.** Most African-American business owners will have to sell to succeed in business. If you have plenty of time and no money, doing the marketing yourself is the lowest "out of pocket" cost method of marketing. Out of pocket costs are the actual dollars you have to spend. Doing the marketing yourself will keep you from spending this money and can also be quite effective.

No one is more familiar with or excited about your product than you. Your knowledge and enthusiasm will help to convince your customers that your product is the one to buy. In the early stages of your business develop, your company will need to concentrate heavily on marketing, and you should to lead the effort. As your company grows, you may want to consider other methods of marketing. Even when you begin to use some of the other methods, never stop marketing your company yourself.

**2) Use other motivated people.** If you have no time and no money, using other people to market your product can be a great option. Many part-time business owners do not have the time to market their company themselves. It's best to enlist people who are willing to sell your product for commission only.

Commission only means the marketing person receives a percentage of the revenue or profit you make on the things they sell. Some of the best salespeople I know only want to sell if they can be on commission only. These professional marketing people realize that they can have unlimited income by selling this way. The more they sell the more they make.

Look for salesmen who are selling other products. People selling related or even competing products can be a good source of marketing manpower for your business. These people are motivated to sell your product because they are only paid when they sell. You will want to track the progress of your new marketing representatives.

You want them to have all the support they need to sell your product. They may need education, demonstration equipment, or lists of potential customers. Make sure they are really motivated to sell your product. Ask about the other products they sell. Be sure your product will not get lost among other products the salesman may be compensated at a higher rate to sell.

Be sure to interview the salesperson. Is her image one you want associated with your product? Ask about his sales record. Check references. It is not uncommon for sales people to change jobs frequently. You will probably want a person with a solid track record. Ask how she plans to market your product. Get a written contract that details the structure of your relationship. Include the length of the contract, the percentage of commission, and the timing of the compensation. Consult your attorney for the details of putting this agreement together.

Using professional marketing people is an outstanding marketing method for many types of high priced products or services. Products that require an explanation, demonstration or direct customer contact are good candidates for using a motivated sales person. It is also a good approach for items that tend to sell in high volume like commercial paper products and industrial equipment or services.

**3) Find free advertising.** There are many places that provide space for free advertising. For example, church bulletin boards are a good source of free advertising space. If your target market can be found in church, use the bulletin board to market. Most of us only consider the bulletin board in our church. Every black church I have ever been in has a bulletin board. If you think it will help, use them all. By the way, white churches have bulletin boards too.

You can also volunteer to work on community dinner committees, trade shows and special programs in exchange for having your name and company name in the program book or mentioned during the program. These events will get you exposure. If you serve a significant role, you will also get a certain level of credibility. Align yourself with quality programs that people respect. You will become associated with this quality and your business will receive the benefits.

Consider attending local and regional civic activities. Be active in meeting people. Smile and try to relax. Your level of confidence will increase the more often you are in these settings. Always carry business cards and talk to as many people as possible. Make sure people know who you are and what you do. Be sincere and friendly. Practice what you will say before you attend these sessions. You want to be sure you appear to know what you are talking about.

Marketing in the civic environment is a great approach for small service companies such as print shops, consultants, accountants, and lawyers. Caterers, retailers, financial planners and insurance representatives should also do well here. Exposure is the name of the game in these businesses, and this strategy is geared to give you and your company the best type of exposure possible—free exposure.

Two other ways to get free marketing exposure are writing articles and creating press releases. You can get your name in circulation by writing articles on subjects in your area of expertise. Submit them to local magazines and newspapers. Assuming the information in the articles is good, you will also become recognized as an authority in your specialty.

Your writing skills can also help your company grow by writing press releases for radio, television, and newspapers. Since these news services will probably not come to you, you will have to take your information to them. Write press releases to announce major happenings with your business.

When you add a new employee, announce it to the public in the form of a press release. If you are ready to start selling a new product, a press release is a way to let other people know of your new plans. New business partnerships, large contracts, and company awards are all good reasons to prepare a press release. Your local library has books on how you can produce effective press releases.

**4) Go door to door.** If you have a lot of time and little money, marketing door-to-door may be an effective strategy. This marketing strategy works well for domestic service businesses such as lawn care, maid services, grocery store delivery and handyman services. This works poorly for commercial services such as computer repair, copier sales and temporary employment services.

Approach door-to-door marketing the same way that you approach mass mail marketing. The major difference is you will probably not have a list of names. You should pick neighborhoods that you think will want and can pay for your services. Everyday in our neighborhood there are signs of door-to-door marketing. Lawn care, realty companies and carpet cleaning companies leave flyers, newsletters and other marketing material hanging on our mail box.

One realtor in my neighborhood got creative in his marketing. He decided to place his flyer along with a plastic American flag next to every mailbox in the neighborhood. His material instructed us to show our patriotism by displaying our new flags on Flag Day and Independence day. When I came home the day he left his flyers, the street was lined with American flags. Of course I wondered what the flags were about. He had achieved his objective. The only way to discover the reason for the flags was to read his marketing material. He just about guaranteed that everyone would see his name and the name of his realty company.

Be creative. Do not be afraid to try new ideas. The object is to get the recipient to read the marketing material. Design a half sheet flyer advertising your company's product or service. The flyer should stress the benefits to the customer of using your company. Benefits like saving money and outstanding results are common winners on marketing flyers. Use the same tips from the mass mailing section to create the material.

Gather your children or those from the neighborhood and

deliver your flyers door-to-door to your potential clients. Find ways to attach the material to the house door or on the outside of the mail box. Practice your delivery method with your troops. Instruct them not to walk through people's grass. It is not a good idea to enter anyone's home to deliver the material. The keys to having an effective door-to-door campaign are to have a good marketing flyer, knowing what doors to place the flyers on, and running the campaign repeatedly. They may not need your service now, but if you are persistent, people will think of you when they do have a need.

**5) Work conferences.** If you are aware of the target market for your product, you can use this information to meet your customers where they gather in large numbers. For example, if your company markets a Christian newsletter for African-Americans, your target market is probably black Christians.

Develop a list of places where your target market gets together. Obvious places are local and state church functions and national conferences. These events are great marketing opportunities because they enable you to maximize the effectiveness of the time you spend. It would take you months of time or thousands of dollars to reach the number of people you can reach in just one or two days at the right conference.

Find out the dates for upcoming national conferences for your target market. You can be sure to find your potential customers there. This is target marketing in the simplest and cheapest form. Someone else has already contacted and got your market together for you. You will not have to go through the expense of sending mailers or making telephone calls to make people aware of your product.

Make contact with the conference promoters and position your business as a vendor. Be prepared to compete with other vendors for the time and attention of the convention participants. Also keep in mind that convention goers come to conventions prepared to spend money. Being a vendor at these sessions can be costly but the benefits can be outstanding.

Conference marketing works best with low to medium price consumer goods. Items such as tapes, books, and T-shirts will all do well. As a general rule, commercial products are purchased based on a relationship and will require a more personal direct marketing strategy, but important contacts can be made at conferences that attract decision makers from commercial prospects. You can then follow-up on these contacts and continue the marketing process.

The consumer market (personal purchases) is built less on relationship and more on awareness and perceived value. If the conference attendees make up your target market, then your product is one that will do well in this environment. Visit your local library and put together a list of associations and groups that support customers in your market.

Effective marketing is part science and part art. Use the tips from this chapter to match your product with a marketing method that is appropriate for your type of business, your time, and your budget. The key is to have a marketing plan that is proactive. Waiting for the customer to come to you could be a long wait.

# *Part IV:*
# *Going for Growth—How Will You Get More Customers?*

Many business owners want to grow their businesses bigger. When we think of bigger, we generally think of more revenue and more employees. **When it comes to business growth, bigger is not always better.** You will want to understand what growth will do to your business. This section discusses growth, adding employees, and needed growth systems. It will help you to understand what it will take to grow your business successfully.

*11*

# *Strategies for Growth*

*"....everywhere and in all things I am instructed both to be full and to be hungry, both to abound and to suffer need."*
—Philippians 4:12

*T*he most simple growth strategies are those that you can perform **within your own business.** These methods are called **internal growth strategies**. When most people think of business growth, they think of getting more customers to buy their present product or service. Growth through adding more customers is the most common growth strategy in all of business.

To accomplish growth through gaining more customers requires some thought. What new customers are you after? How do you plan to get them? To succeed with this strategy, you will have to revisit your original marketing plan and realign it to include your new group of customers. **Simply doing more marketing will not necessarily attract more customers. In an effort to attract more customers, business owners begin to do more marketing without knowing where those new customers will come from.** Although this method seems simple and easy, there are limits to the amount of growth you can achieve by merely adding new customers.

Think of the customers who buy your product or the product of one of your competitors as pieces of a pie. You and your competitors have already sliced the pie into a particular number of pieces. Since there is only one pie, making your piece larger will mean making your competitor's piece smaller. You can steal the pie of others during your introduction into the market place.

**Once your company is a known commodity, the size of your piece of pie will become established or fixed. You will continue to take pie from others but they will take an equal amount of pie from you.** Your business growth will level off. Your potential for additional growth through new customers is now limited.

Also keep in mind that adding new customers for the sole purpose of growth often hurts the profits of a growing business. In an effort to attract new customers, some companies relax credit terms or lower prices. Although revenue grows, profit and cash flow suffer. New customers can also bring poor payment patterns. Slow paying customers will hurt cash flow and profits.

Growth is important to your business, but you must think through your growth strategy. Always look for new customers, but make sure they are customers you really want. **You want to give your bad customers to your competition and spend your time taking their good ones.**

There are other internal growth strategies that you can use to overcome the limits placed on the growth potential of your business. **Internal growth focuses on generating more business from the present assets (skills, intelligence, equipment, experience, etc.) of the company.** Making a new product or service from a present product is a common internal growth strategy. Look at the products and services you now provide. Are there uses for these products other than those presently being marketed?

Also consider adding products to your service. For example, if you own a cleaning service company, you may want to begin selling cleaning products. You already know the benefits and drawbacks of each product. Although selling the product means acquiring new skills, it is still related to your present business.

Service companies are often geographically limited because there is only so far you can afford to travel to perform your service. On the other hand, you can market and sell your product anywhere. This opens the door to unlimited opportunity.

This growth method can also work in reverse. You can also add services to your product. A distributor for fax machine equipment can add fax repair services to the existing line of equipment sales. Your satisfied fax machine customers will be great prospects for your new repair service. After all, customers you know are the best customers to have. Adding services to your product, or vice versa, will allow for growth without the uncertainty of dealing with new customers.

Another internal growth strategy is **forward and backward integration. Integration is adding to your product line the product or services of the suppliers you buy from and/ or the wholesalers you sell to.** When this strategy is done well, it can increase profits, improve responsiveness, and give you better control of your business.

For example, a business owner from Indiana was a distributor of greeting cards. She contracted with card manufacturers to produce cards that her company distributed to local card shops throughout the country. Poor quality cards and rising prices from card manufactures convinced this business owner to pursue making the greeting cards herself. She also felt she could make more money by avoiding local card shops and selling her new greeting cards directly to the end customer.

After investigating her new idea more fully, she was ready to implement both forward and backward integration (Figure 11.1). In order to own the complete process, she needed to make the cards and distribute them directly to the end user. She used subcontractors to develop and manufacture greeting cards to her specifications.

### Figure 11.1. Forward and Backward Integration

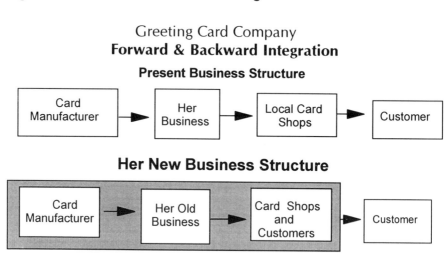

Greeting Card Company
**Forward & Backward Integration**
**Present Business Structure**

**Her New Business Structure**

In addition, she contracted with a mail order company to sell her products through the mail. The business still buys some cards from other manufacturers, and she still sells cards to the same retail shops that she had done business with in the past. The difference is that she no longer depends on any one source to make and sell her product. She has also improved both profit and control in her business.

By implementing forward and backward integration, you will increase profits because you will be able to keep the profits that you used to give to your suppliers as well as the profits your wholesalers used to get when they sold to the distributors or the consumer. You will also be able to respond better to your customers. No more waiting for delivery from your supplier. You will control all aspects of the supplier channel. Price, delivery, and quality will now be a part of your company.

**It is also possible to use your intellectual capital or brain power as an actual product.** Will people pay for your knowledge? Do not underestimate what you know and how it may be of value to others. What comes easy to you, may be very difficult for others. What you believe is common knowledge may not be so common to someone else. Selling what you know about your business can be a very sound growth idea. **The object is to fully use all of the assets in your company. The brain power of your company is often a very significant asset.** Consider things your firm does better than anyone else. Think about special processes or unique management styles used in your business.

While internal growth is the most common growth strategy used by African-American business owners, many of us are ready to use external growth strategies. Growing your company by external means involves connecting your company to another company through some type of business arrangement.

The most common arrangements are business mergers or business acquisitions. Mergers and acquisitions can be quite complex and are beyond the scope of this book. To be certain that you approach external growth strategies properly, seek the advice of an attorney with experience in this area.

*12*

# Growth Can Kill Your Business

*"Milk the cow, but don't pull off the udder."*
—M. Tupper

*W*e have all seen small business owners who spend every waking moment working in their businesses. They are always on site performing or personally overseeing every aspect of the day-to-day work. The business does well. Quality is high, and customer service is good. Customers enjoy their experience with this company, word spreads, and the business begins to grow rapidly. In attempting to keep up with the increased business demand, the business owner begins to add employees. As the owner tries to do more and more, the likelihood of error increases.

The massive work hours begin to impact the business owner's health, personal life, and business outlook. He has not been in business long enough to reap the benefits from his efforts. Many business owners become disenchanted with entrepreneurship. The amount of work the owner must perform often becomes overwhelming. **African-American business owners are often "worked out" of business.**

When the business owner does add personnel, the new employees have different work habits and pay less attention to customer service. Since the business owner can no longer oversee each work activity, quality declines. Customer complaints increase, and customers begin to have negative experiences with the company. Business begins to slow down.

No one realizes it at the time, but the African-American business owner has grown himself out of business. If the business had stayed small enough for the owner to run alone, it would still be in business. The business owner blames the demise of the business on lack of support from the black community or the racist system. Growth is often the real business killer.

This situation does not have to happen. Earlier in the book, I mentioned the difference between business technicians and business entrepreneurs (See introduction to get more information on the traits of entrepreneurs). Business technicians get into business to be independent and provide a jobs for themselves. Whereas entrepreneurs get into business to increase their wealth, create jobs, and leave a business legacy.

A business technician's company is not designed to grow at a rapid rate. Growth will be more gradual and limited by the work capacity of the business owner. Entrepreneurs specifically structure their businesses for growth. They build business systems that will support the growth they desire. (See Chapter 13 for more detail on building a growth system.) An entrepreneur hopes to build a business in which she will one day not work. If you are an African- American business person, you must think like an entrepreneur.

One must always think about the systems of the business. The term systems simply means the method or way things should be done. Documenting this system will give everyone the same understanding of the processes of your business. Whether the business owner is present or not, the system will make it possible for the workers to know what they should be doing.

Creating a business system will take some effort in the beginning, but the alternative is living with the results of growing a business with no systems. Established systems will position your company to perform with or without you.

Spend the time in the beginning. You will need to continually fine tune your systems as the needs of your business change. If you know about your business, building your company's business systems will be fairly simple. The chapters that follow will discuss ways to successfully grow your new business and avoid many of the pitfalls that often hinder small businesses.

# 13

# *Building Your Growth System*

*"It's not the load that breaks you down, it's the way you carry it."*

—Lena Horne, Singer

*T*o an entrepreneur, every business is the same. General construction is viewed the same as a restaurant, and consulting is the same as trucking. **The key to growing any entrepreneurial business for long-term stability is to establish well thought out business systems.** Building your business systems is as easy as a a 3-step process that may cost you nothing or very little to put together:

**Step 1: Layout your business like an assembly line.** Look at everything involved in the process of running your business. Start with the customer who should be the end point of the process. Trace each step backward from getting paid by the customer all the way through to buying your materials from your suppliers. Your process should start with the customer because you will want the rest of the steps to support the total satisfaction of your customer. Be sure to include all of the items in the process. This step will help you get a visual picture of the components in your business. It will force you to think of all the steps needed to create, deliver, and get payment for your particular service or product.

**Step 2: Break down each phase of the process into steps within the phase.** One of the phases in your business will probably be billing your clients for the products or services they have received. Potential steps in this phase are determining billing amount, printing customer invoices, mailing the invoice and following up on unpaid bills.

For example, we thought we had a good billing system at our engineering company. For the first two and half years, we were able to bill customers accurately and receive payment in a timely manner. Mid-way through our third year of business, we experienced tremendous growth. More customer activity began to show us flaws in our billing system.

We started billing customers inaccurately and our accounts receivable account (money people owed to us) began to grow. These two problems caused customer satisfaction issues and poor cash flow. So almost three years after we established the original system, we began to see the steps we had missed.

You will have to look at each phase and determine the needed steps. This is an ongoing process, and you should not expect to be able to layout each step in each phase right away. Put your energy into getting the process started. Don't worry about the ones you miss. Other steps will become evident as you continue to grow as a business.

When you believe you have documented each step, begin to look for steps that may not be needed. Look for items that are duplicates of others. Can you not do something in the process and still get the work done and keep the customer satisfied? Steps put in place just for checking the work of others are good candidates for removal. Everyone should be responsible for the quality of their own work. Simplifying your steps will give your personnel less to do, and they will have more time to increase their productivity. With less to think about, it will be easier to encourage people to use the systems.

**Step 3: Determine the best way to perform the steps you outlined above.** How will the way you do one step effect the other steps? What steps can be automated by any equipment or computers you may have? Be specific and leave nothing to the imagination.

Things as simple as how the telephone should be answered are important items that should be documented in your systems. If everyone knows you answer the telephone with the company name and your personal name, no one will answer the telephone with a simple "hello." You want everyone involved with your business to understand the instructions in the same way.

In addition to standardization, automation may also help to increase productivity, improve your systems, and provide some of the checks and balances that your business may need. Look at your systems for areas that may be done more efficiently by automation. Does your system have steps that require standard calculations?

Accounting, payroll management, billing, and project management are usually areas where automation can be easily used. Consult Chapter 27 for more detail on using technology to improve your business. Before you make any changes in your present systems, consult Chapter 16 to be sure your changes will not negatively effect your business or your customer.

**The objective of a growth system is to operate your business as efficiently and consistently as possible.** Everyone associated with your business should do things in a common fashion every time. You should act as if you will not be around to tell people what must be done. Make sure your instructions are clear enough so that people will be able to do things the way that you want them done. Ask any current employees for their input. If you have no established business systems, business growth will begin to show the weaknesses of the individuals in your company.

Lay your business out like an assembly line. Break down each phase of the process into steps within the phase, and then determine the best way to perform the steps that you have outlined.

The three steps to an effective growth system discussed in this chapter will help your company deal positively with growth. You, your employees, and especially your customers have to know what to expect. Put the right systems in place and enjoy the great feeling of a growing business.

14

# Growing Your Staff

*"Buy wisdom, and instruction, and understanding."*
—Solomon

*N*ow that your business growth systems are in place, it is time to bring in the additional personnel that you will need to grow your company. Selecting personnel can be a very complex and exhausting process. For African-American business owners, the added pressure of feeling the need to find black employees makes this process all the more involved.

This publication will give you a basic understanding of the issues related to hiring employees, but it is not a substitute for doing more in-depth reading on the subject. Do not let personnel issues slow you down. Utilize the strategies suggested here, ask for input from others, and then do something.

There is no substitute for experience, and this rule is especially true when making human resource decisions. All people, situations, and businesses are different. Your own experience will be your ultimate education.

Issues of money and diversity must be thought through before you can even start the actual hiring process. How much money you have to spend on the talent you need is an important number to know. Establish the number before you start. If you wait until you find the right candidate for the job you may be tempted to offer more to be sure the person accepts your offer. Set the salary or hourly rate up front. Then seek out a person that meets your needs and your budget.

The importance of the diversity of your work force is determined by your personal style. Some African-American business owners do not consider the racial mix of employees when selecting their staff. They look for the best candidate for the position at the time. Others only hire African-Americans.

One reason for this that African-American people are the people we know and with whom we feel most comfortable. Another reason for only hiring black employees is that business owners feel an obligation to give "our people" a chance. These business owners believe that black-owned companies should only have black employees. The racial mix you select is obviously up to you. It is your company, and your beliefs are the beliefs that are important.

I believe that you need a diverse workforce to be successful. You will need people of different races, backgrounds, and education levels; but do not forget people of different sexes, ages, and religions. The mix of these diverse groups directed at common objectives will position your company to take advantage of all opportunities in the marketplace. Your customers will probably be from a cross section of the population.

The more you and your staff know about these different groups the more effective your company will be in meeting their unique needs. A diverse work group is important and worth the extra effort to obtain, but selecting a person for any other reason than their skills will hurt your business. If your business is hurt too much and too often, it will not be able to survive. If you are not in business, you will not be able to provide opportunities for anyone. Always keep the good of the business clear in your mind. Give people a chance when you can and when they deserve it.

## Evaluating Employee Skills

Once your mind is made up on the amount of money you can offer and any diversity considerations you may have, you are ready to begin the process of finding the right person for your job opening. Determining what you need is the first step in bringing on the right skill. What skills are required to perform the needed tasks? Skills are the human behaviors that you can test.

Examples of skills are using a particular word processor, operating a specific type of construction equipment, or understanding the accounting needs of a small business. These skills are also called tangible attributes because they are abilities that you can observe.

Look at a person's past experience, education, and recommendations to get a quick feel for their skills. Don't overlook people who are young or trying to switch careers. These people will often work harder and be more flexible than more experienced workers. They may also be less expensive to hire.

High personnel costs are a major contributor to business failure. Hiring flexible workers will help you hold down your personnel expenses and still meet the dynamic needs of your customers. The more flexible your employees, the more they will able to do. This will allow you to hire fewer people and provide more stable work for those you do hire.

If you are looking for a painter, roofer, and a carpenter,

try to find one person who can do all of these jobs. This will give you flexibility in using the person in many situations. When your roofing work is slow, the person can paint or do carpentry. Employees who are not flexible will spend idle time doing nothing and probably cost you money.

Your employee needs will surely involve multiple skills. Since these skills that you need may all seem equally important, rank the skills by listing them from most important to least important. The prioritized list will help you select the top candidate for the job. But you will have to decide which are the skills your company cannot do without and identify the skills you are able to train to increase them to the level needed for the job.

For those people you find that have the needed skills, you will want to decide what traits are important. Traits are intangible items that are almost impossible to measure. Items such as honesty, motivation, attitude, and ability to work with others are all personal traits.

Your new employee's success will be determined more on these traits than on their actual skills. Great cooks who cannot be trusted around the cash register will not succeed in your business. If the employment candidate is unable to work with others in the company, it will be difficult to fully utilize their skills.

You should approach the intangible traits in the same way that you decided on the tangible skills. List the intangible traits most important to you and your business. Rank them in order of their importance. An example of a skills and traits list is shown in Figure 14.1.

## Where Do You Find the People You Need?

Since you already know what type of person you are looking for, you simply need to look in the right places. If you think of looking for an employee in the same way as looking

**Figure 14.1. Examples of Skills and Traits of Potential Employees**

| Skills | Traits |
| --- | --- |
| Bookkeeping | Honesty |
| Typing | Flexibility |
| Mechanic | Loyalty |
| Carpentry | Communication |
| Computers | Attitude |
| Painting | Self Starter |
| Roofing | Dependability |
| Cooking | Leadership |

for a job, it will be much easier to go through the process. The first place to look for potential employees is with the people you know. Tell your friends and relatives you are trying to fill a new position. Be sure to tell them the skills and traits the position requires. Your associates will almost always know people who can fill your employment need.

These candidates may or may not have the skills you need. You must be ready to reject people recommended to you by your friends. When you receive a name from someone, ask if the person has the skills and traits you need. If they do not, thank the person for the lead, but let them know the person does not fit what you want.

Places where you have worked and former co-workers are another source of good employees. You may even know these people personally. You will be in a position to know what actual skills and traits they possess. You know if they come to work everyday and if they can work with others.

I went back to my former employer IBM to find an office manager for our first engineering office. The primary skill needed was a solid background in the use of computer software. I had seen the skills and traits firsthand and felt comfortable hiring the person away from IBM. Hiring someone you used to work with is like having the privilege of seeing a person in a prolonged interview.

Church is also a place to get leads for good employees. Take a look around your church. Talk to your minister. Ask about people who may be looking for work. Post a job description on the church bulletin board. **For small growing businesses, open job advertising should be a last resort.** Having employees you can trust is very important during the early stages of a company's growth.

Open advertising and hiring will increase your chances of getting someone that will cause you problems. It is also expensive both in terms of the cost of advertising and the time spent sorting through the many responses you will surely receive. **Try all of the search techniques that involve people you know. Give these search methods a fair chance to work for you.** If you hit a brick wall, consider using traditional employee search methods.

Tread lightly and be sure the person you hire is all that she appears to be. Few people make their resumes look bad, so be sure to check references. Do background checks and maybe give a skills test. Do whatever it takes to be sure you have gotten what you need.

## What About Hiring Relatives and Friends?

African-American business owners often select employees based on things other than the skills needed to be successful in business. We often make decisions to hire relatives because we do not have the money to pay "real" employees. We may hire friends because they deserve a chance or need a job. These are lofty ideas, but the success of the business is also important.

Your business must succeed or you and your friends and

relatives will be without jobs. Providing employment for their families is the dream of many black business owners. Keeping things in the family is great as long as your business is benefiting from the addition of your relatives. Relatives and friends often make great employees, but African-American businesses sometimes suffer greatly because of hiring under-qualified friends and relatives.

Our company was doing business with a company in Cleveland, Ohio. The business owners were quite skilled in their professions. They were very busy and often difficult to contact by telephone, so they had a receptionist/office manager to run the office while they were out. Each time we called the office we met with the same response.

The receptionist was always rude, short, and hard to deal with. She never wanted to give us any information, and we always felt we were inconveniencing her with our telephone call.

After dealing with this issue for several months, we finally had the opportunity to meet with the owners at their office. When we entered, the president of the company introduced my partner and I to his sister, the receptionist and office manager. In my opinion, she did not have the skills and traits needed for this position. We completed the work we were doing with that company, and we never called them again. What if all of their customers did the same thing? They would soon be out of business.

Hiring your relatives and friends is tempting. Before you hire your buddy or your cousin always ask two key questions. First, do they have the skills and traits you would look for in any other person? Second, do they add value to your company? Will the business be better off with them than without them? If the answers to these questions are yes, then hiring your friend or relative is a major advantage. If the answer is no, do not put your business in jeopardy.

Hiring people is one of the most difficult aspects of running your own business. Since you cannot do all of the work forever, you must learn to select employees as best you can. Using these tips as a guide will help, but the bottom line is always: "Does the person add value to your company?" If he does add value, then chances are good that you have made a good decision. If she does not add value, the employee's other traits will not matter. They must add something to the business.

*15*

# Good Customer Service Is a Gold Mine

*"Remember... the customer is always king"*
—Unknown

*M*y interviews with African-American business owners show that a lack of customer satisfaction is a key reason for the failure of black-owned businesses. If all of your customers were satisfied, they would all come back, and they would also refer others to your business. You would continue to sell your product or service to your current customers, and your business would grow from the new customers referred to you by the old ones. This customer service concept can be a gold mine.

A few years ago, I attempted to develop a simple calculation that would show how much a single customer would be worth to my engineering consulting company. The calculation started with an average customer deal size of $30,000. The average deal size for our company was really $50,000, but we used $30,000 in the calculation to make the answer a conservative estimate.

If the client hired our firm once a year for 15 years, this

client generated $450,000 in revenue. Based on our company profit objective of 25%, the client was worth over $112,500 of profit. And this was only one client. What about the people she tells about our outstanding service? What will they be worth?

Satisfied clients grow exponentially. The process works as follows: One satisfied customer tells three others. (Some say a satisfied customer tells between 7 and 10 others). These three come to your business and become satisfied customers. Each of them goes out and tells three more people. These nine people once satisfied with your product tell three others.

This short example shows how a business can yield 39 new customers just by satisfying the first. The value of a single satisfied customer is shown graphically in figure 15.1. These clients were secured with no additional marketing or advertising dollars. In case you were wondering, the cost of bad customer service will kill your business faster than good customer service will help. Instead of telling three people about your service, a dissatisfied customer will tell as many as 11 people.

Do the numbers for your business. You can't afford not to invest in customer satisfaction. It is actually the most cost effective marketing you can have.

What do you think of when you hear the words 'customer service'? Most people think of people smiling, saying thank you or delivering a hardy hello. Most of us expect to be waited on promptly and greeted courteously. This treatment is not seen as anything special. In fact, it is seen as mandatory.

Customer service in minority businesses is often the root of many negative image and perception problems. Customer service must be seen as a part of our product or service. If your business is going to gain acceptance, you will have to

## Figure 15.1. The Power of One Satisfied Customer

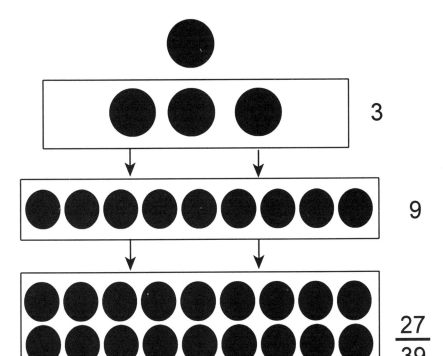

put together your own system for taking care of your customers. There is only one measure of the success of customer service: Is the customer satisfied? The kind words and gestures are just window dressing. Customer service must go farther.

Our company was considering joining a private dinner club. We wanted to use the club to entertain our clients at lunch, dinner and formal meetings. As I spoke with the associate in charge of membership, she began to sell me on the benefits of club membership. She talked about our free access to any of the plush meeting rooms in the club. She was careful to mention that I could use all member clubs in major U.S. cities. She spoke of the outstanding food quality and the overall attention to detail.

The club takes pride in recognizing the members and calling them by name: "We try to call each member by name at least three times" she said. Well I went for it. The price was right and the benefits seemed worth my company's investment. My first meal at the club was  breakfast with another local businessman.

The membership coordinator was right. The food quality was exceptional, and the atmosphere was conducive to discussing business. But when my cup of coffee was empty, I could not get the cup refilled. Waiters and waitresses passed our table without even a glance. What was going on? Thirty minutes later when I had completed my breakfast and my business, my guest and I left.

Although they mentioned my name three times and served great food, what I remembered most was that I could not get a second cup of the best coffee that I had ever tasted. Drop all of the non-important customer service gimmicks. If your company is going to build a strong image and overcome the standard barriers confronting African-American businesses, you must be serious about real customer service.

Follow the steps outline in the next section. Reach out to your clients and provide them with customer service on their terms.

## *Five Steps to Happy Customers*

**1) Determine what the customer wants.** Never assume you know what your customer wants. Always ask. Ask gently, but ask often. You never want to force your clients to give you feedback, but always make the option available and convenient. Consider using surveys. Point of sale surveys work the best. While you are adding up the customer's bill, ask them to complete a short (three question) survey.

Use the survey to find out how you are doing. Ask about the issues most important to them. Timeliness, quality of service, price—they all can be evaluated. If you send your bills by mail, include your survey in the mailing. Your rate of response will not be as high as surveys delivered in person, but the information returned will be just as good.

Many companies survey customers by telephone. Make sure these calls are short, sweet, and to the point. A maximum of three questions in a customer service telephone survey is all you should ask your customer to answer. The total telephone call should take less than a minute.

If you go too far, you risk annoying the customer. None of us likes getting telephone calls at home. They always come while we are eating dinner or helping our children with their homework. There is no good time to call a person for customer satisfaction information. But if the calls are done well and take very little time, most customers will not mind.

My daughter's dentist is good at follow-up telephone calls. She once extracted a number of my daughter's teeth in preparation for dental braces. That evening she called personally (It would have meant less if someone else from her office had called.) and asked for my daughter. She asked how she was doing. She wanted to be sure that the bleeding had stopped, and there was no serious pain. My daughter felt important, and we were impressed.

If there was something wrong, we would have called the dentist, but by her calling us, she was building our customer satisfaction. She knows her patients want a dentist who is concerned with their well being. By the way, based on that one minute telephone call, I recommended a friend to her practice. The telephone call took some of her time and clearly cost her something, but a satisfied customer is priceless.

**2) Give the customer what they want.** You have asked your customers to express their desires. You must now have the trust to give them what they want. You are going to have to trust that the benefits of your extra effort will bring you worthwhile returns. For a year, I tried to convince a local physician to ask her patients what they wanted in a physician.

Convenience is one of the important criteria for most folks when they go to the doctor. Will they be seen on time? Do the office hours fit the schedule of the patient? Is the office staff courteous and helpful? Do the physicians spend enough time with the patients? This doctor was not comfortable asking these questions because she was not sure she was willing to act on the patient's input.

What if they want Saturday and evening hours? Or they expected the doctors to spend more time with them? I agreed, these desires would mean more work for the three physicians in her office. But what if the new hours and additional attention meant a thirty percent increase in patient load? Would this additional business be enough of a return to justify the extra effort? The issue is one of trust.

The three physicians in this office must decide how they can give the customers what they want and still personally enjoy a quality standard of living. They must begin to see their patients as customers. You will have to do the same if you are serious about customer satisfaction.

**3) Make customer service everyone's job.** A customer measures his level of service based on his contact with everyone that he meets in your business. One solution is for you to handle each customer yourself. Of course you would treat every customer well and customer satisfaction would be high. The problem with this approach is obvious. Your business could only grow as large as the number of customers that you could handle personally.

Many black entrepreneurs are practicing "the one man customer satisfaction team." They are at their business location constantly. They attempt to handle every issue of the business personally. This method will not work if the goal of the business is to grow. Some black business owners bet their marriages, health and business futures by continuing as a one person show. We become tired of the constant hustle of our business and often close our doors before we have a chance for success.

**Transfer your passion for the business to the people you hire. Make sure they know the importance of customer satisfaction.** Show them how they have the responsibility and power to solve customers concerns. (See the building your systems for growth section in Chapter 13) Then give your people some room to implement customer service techniques.

This will leave you time to concentrate on growing your business beyond the limits of a one person operation. Make sure every person in your business knows that nothing is more important than the customer.

**4) Make a big deal over your mistakes.** You should be physically ill over your company making a mistake. When you are doing a hundred hairdos a week, washing thousands of cars a month or preparing many meals a day, mistakes will happen. No matter what systems you have in place to prevent it, someone's car will not be clean or some customer's dinner will be overcooked. Customers measure customer service based on how you respond to your mistakes. Mistakes seem rare to you because you deal with such high volumes.

But for the customer that only gets one hairdo a month, one mistake is a major problem. Since it is a major problem to them, it must be a major problem to you. The proper response to a mistake is simple but seldom used. First, you apologize. Apologize quickly and sincerely. A verbal apology is usually enough, but if the mistake is major, like you ruined the paint job on a customers car while doing a wax and buff job, you may need to apologize at the next level. Send a letter, flowers or whatever you believe is appropriate.

An apology is not an explanation. The customer does not care that your car technician is new and inexperienced. They don't care that the buffing equipment malfunctioned. They do not want to hear that you have gotten no complaints from other customers. They know they have a problem, and they want it fixed.

The second step to dealing with a mistake is to fix the situation...immediatly. Don't make this customer wait. No matter how busy you are or how much it will cost, their situation must be placed at the front of the line. Let the customer know what you plan to do to correct the situation. Try to find a way not to inconvenience the customer any more than needed. In our example of the poorly buffed car, you may offer to provide a rental car while his car is being re-done.

Offer to bring the completed car to their office or home to avoid another trip to your place of business. If you think this solution is too expensive, you should refer to the beginning of this chapter on the value of a satisfied customer.

**5) Determine the source of the problem and change (or create) your system to prevent the mistake from happening again.** Getting used to mistakes happening is a prescription for a short business life. When a mistake happens, fix it first. Then find out why it happened. Was it a lack of adequate training, a breakdown in your system, or simply a lack of responsibility by someone in your company?

Be sure to find the "root" cause of the problem. Just as with a strong weed in your garden, if you pull off the top and leave the root, the weed or in this case the problem, will come right back. By finding and eliminating the root you will assure this particular problem will not occur again.

As our engineering company became more and more busy, it was increasingly difficult to keep everyone's attention focused on the top priorities of the company. We were forced to rush the completion of projects because the due date would sneak up on us. Our office manager was the only person who had a calendar of all of our business deadlines. Everyone else worked on their present project without much knowledge of other activities coming.

This method finally gave way when we missed a deadline for an important proposal. We promised the customer the proposal on a particular date. Since we could not afford to make this mistake again, we had to find out what happened. Was it our office manager's fault? After all she was the keeper of the only calendar. Was it my fault? I made the commitment to the customer and therefore I should have known the date.

The real problem was the lack of a system that kept the entire office aware of the activities of the company. We developed a system which includes assigning the completion of an activity to an individual and posting a project board on the wall in the office. We have continued to update this system, but the base has remained the same. We now meet our customer deadlines and maintain their confidence in our work.

## Evaluating New Customer Service Ideas

Creating a customer service system will help your company meet the ever changing needs of your customers. By creating a customer service system, you will always be in touch with their wants and desires. Staying close to the customer will keep you ahead of the competition. Whatever your type of business, customer service must be the center of all of your company activity.

If you believe you need a new drill press, you should

wonder how it will impact the customer. Before you change your restaurant menu, you should be sure the customer will not see the change as negative. Every decision in your business should be done with the customer in mind. The following ten questions were developed to help you make sure that the impact of customer service changes on the customer and the business will be positive:

1) What is the advantage to the customer?

2) Will the customer value the advantage?

3) What impact will this idea have on employees?

4) What will be the effect on present systems?

5) Is anyone else doing it successfully? What can we learn from their experience?

6) What could go wrong?

7) Will we gain a sustainable competitive advantage? (See chapter 8 for an explanation of sustainable competitive advantage.)

8) How much money will we have to spend?

9) Is there financial gain for the company?

10) When should we review and evaluate this new idea?

When you have answers to all of these questions, you are ready to decide on any proposed change. Some of these questions could lead you to believe you should make a decision that helps the customer and hurts your company. This is never the case. If your customer wants to continue to get quality products and services from you, you must continue to make a profit. These questions are designed to help you identify situations where both the company and the customer win. These are the situations that will improve your business success and the quality of service to your customers.

Providing good customer service is easy if you always put yourself in the place of the customer. Know what they want and give it to them. Remember good customers refer other customers to your business. A satisfied customer is your business' most valuable asset. Treat them with care.

# Part V:
# Financing Your Business

There are many ways to finance your new business idea. **The most common are self financing, investment partners, banks, and venture capital investment.** Understanding the benefits and pitfalls of these financing methods will help you select the proper financing alternative for your business situation.

# 16

# *Strategies for Self-Financing*

*"There are some countries so backward that their people don't spend money until they have saved it."*

—A.G. Gaston
Entrepreneur

*Y*ou have a great idea for starting your own business. You have refined your product and calculated the proper product price. You know who your customers are and how you will persuade them to do business with you. Only one issue stands in the way of you starting your business; you need money to make your idea a reality. Even the smallest of small businesses needs some start-up money.

Self-financing or using your own money is always a solid method of getting your business started. The benefit of self-financing is that it adds to the value of your company without adding any debt or liability.

No debt will mean your business will have a positive net worth (Net worth is all the things the company owns minus all the bills the company owes or assets minus liabilities). A positive net worth will be important when you grow to a level that demands that you get financing from outside financing sources.

The easiest, fastest and, in some cases, the best method of getting the financing you need is from your personal savings. Whether it is money from early retirement, corporate buyout packages, or a 401k pension plan, you have the most control over your own funds. With this method of self-financing, you can move ahead with your plans without much delay. Although you control this money, it is still a good idea to plan carefully before investing. Hopefully, careful planning will help to avoid you wasting your funds.

What if you do not have a pot of money to use to finance your business? Another self-financing alternative is performing services to get the money you need to start your business. Consulting in an area in which you have expert knowledge is a good service idea.

If you perform services in the area of your business idea, you are actually doing some pre-business marketing. If the people you perform services for enjoy the relationship, then they will respect you when you start your business. Also consider getting a part-time job to earn extra money that you can save for your new business venture.

A third strategy of self-financing your business is to use your personal credit to get money. The key to this method is to use your personal credit and not the credit of the business. An example of personal credit is a home equity loan.

By getting a home equity loan, you can then put the money into the business as equity. This will improve your company's net worth and increase your chances of getting outside financing in the future. The disadvantage of using your own credit is that you personally accrue more debt. More personal debt could limit your family's access to needed money in the future. It may be a good idea to talk to an accountant about this method.

The last and least suggested method of self-financing is to use your personal credit cards. This method of small business financing is very expensive. Most credit card interest rates are much higher than other sources of funds.

Using credit cards, in combination with a good plan to pay the cards off, can be a successful way to launch a new small business. Make this option your last alternative. Credit cards can ruin your personal credit and leave you and your family in real financial trouble. Credit card financing is a risky financing strategy, so proceed with extreme caution.

## Someone Else's Money

If the self financing methods mentioned above do not fit your taste or your financial position, consider using someone else's money. Many business owners get their start-up money from friends and relatives. Getting a financial partner can be an effective idea. Find someone who has the funds you need. In exchange for their contribution of money, you will give this new partner a percentage ownership in the company.

The new partner will get all the benefits of the growth and success of your business, and you will get the benefit of badly needed money. This method of financing is not debt, and therefore, will have a positive impact on your company's net worth.

Getting a financial partner you are familiar with is a great way to get your business started. Although there are many benefits, there are some issues you should consider. Picking a financial partner is almost as important as selecting a partner that will be active in the business.

Do you and your potential partner agree on the company objectives? Have you decided (and documented) the role of your new partner? Decide upfront how the partner will be paid back and when. This is not a situation to be taken lightly. Have an attorney develop any contractual agreements. Look to friends, family members, churches and local business people as potential business partners or investors. Be ready to convince your potential partners. You will need a strong plan and a professional presentation in order to convince individuals that they should invest their money in your business.

Private investors or partners that you know are the best source of financing if you do not have the money yourself. **The African-American community has the money to start businesses.** Starting businesses represents our opportunity to finance our own firms and recycle our funds in our own interest. Making the private investment method work will require paying close attention to the details of your agreement.

Consider these financing methods first before you go to an outside source for money. African-American business owners often apply for outside financing too early in the development of their companies. A friend and business financial consultant says, "The person holding the debt owns the business."

If you get a loan from a bank to start your business, the bank now has ownership. He likened it to getting a loan for the purchase of a car or a house. Until you pay off the loan, the bank holds the title to your car and the mortgage to your home. Self financing can grow your business to a point that will make it more attractive to outside financing companies. Bottomline, try to finance your business with funds close to home.

If you have trouble convincing others to invest money into your business, you may want to take a closer look at your business idea. If you have explained your idea well and no one wants to invest, your idea may not be as good as you thought. Review your total concept. If no one wants to invest their money, perhaps you should not be investing your time.

## 17

# Bank Financing

*"Sooner or later we've got to polish ourselves up; we've got to let the shine come through."*

—Lou Rawls,
Singer

## What's going on at the bank?

Bank financing is the second most common source of business financing. African-American business owners often have a tough time obtaining money from banks. Part of the problem is the bank's traditional view of black businesses. The other part of the problem is our lack of understanding of what the bank wants.

We should continue to push for improvement in the rate of success that black businesses have with the banking industry. However, we should also improve our knowledge and general understanding of banks and bank financing.

It is a fact that black business owners often have a tough time getting bank financing. With this in mind, we must develop strategies to work around the normal barriers and get the bank to say "yes."

**The single most misunderstood fact about banks is the nature of their business objectives.** Banks are in the business of making money. They make money by granting loans. Banks are successful if they are able to do two things. First, they must actually grant loans. If they do not grant loans, they will not be successful as a bank. Granting loans only means they have an opportunity to make money.

Second, to make money, they must also get the loans paid back. If the loans are not paid back, the bank cannot make a profit. Although the function of the bank is to grant loans and get them paid back, there are many additional issues involved in the bank process.

Another facet of the bank system is the institutional racism that exists in the industry. The term institutional racism was selected on purpose because the racism is allowed as a part of the bank system. As long as there is no set criteria for approving or denying loans, people will continue to be treated unfairly. The present bank systems allow for equal loan applications to be treated in different ways.

Loans are approved or denied based on something as subjective as the character of the applicant. We are not going to change the system overnight. Unless we want to defer our dream until the banking climate is more to our liking, we must begin to prepare ourselves to operate within the present system.

We, as the African-American business community, must begin to focus on **structuring our businesses** so the banking industry will be more accepting. We must prepare our businesses to operate successfully the way things are today.

## What Does the Bank Want from You?

When you approach the bank for financing, you will **personally** need to be prepared to support your business.

Unless your business has been around for many years and has a strong credit history of its own, it will be your personal credit that the bank will look at most. Be prepared to show the following personal information to the bank when you apply for business financing:

**1) Ability to repay the loan** - If your business fails, can you personally repay the money your business has borrowed?

**2) Something as collateral** - House, investments, equipment.

**3) Good personal credit** - The bank wants to know if you pay your bills on time.

**4) Personal Guarantee** - You will have to sign personal responsibility to the loan. (If you are married, your spouse may also be asked to sign)

**5) Business background** - The bank will want to know if you have the skills to run the business you have chosen.

Document everything, and do your best to describe why you are the right person to run the company you are presenting. Our first business loan involved pledging the personal residences of my partner and myself. We also had to have our spouses sign the loan for additional insurance. If you go to the bank, have your act together. The better your professional image, the better your position will be. Always remember, banks want guaranteed repayment.

## What Does the Bank Want from Your Business?

Your personal history is very important when you first apply for business financing, but do not underestimate the importance of sound, thorough business information. The bank will have a better impression of your business and your business skills if you have your information prepared. The businesses that the bank wants to give loans to will meet the following criteria:

1) 3 to 5 Years of Revenue Growth
2) Positive Company Net Worth
3) Comprehensive Business Plan
4) Company Profits

If you do not have all these requirements, do not be discouraged. Prepare what you have and explain your position. A start-up company cannot have all of the items that a bank will want to see. If your presentation is good enough, it is possible to get bank financing anyway.

## Getting the Bank to Say "Yes"

There are several things that you can do to improve your chances of being getting bank financing. **Build multiple bank relationships early in the life of your business.** Whether you need money or not, you need to make the contacts early.

Explain your business to the multiple potential bankers. Show them your business plan and financial projections. Help them understand when you plan to make a profit. Describe your marketing plan and explain your competitive advantage.

After your initial meeting, continue to keep the contacts aware of your company's progress. Consider creating a quarterly press release. List new contracts, markets, clients, and products. You will want to state your financial position and give the bankers an idea of your financial future. This communication allows you to document your progress on a regular basis. This information will be helpful when you actually need to make your move for bank financing.

When you are ready to approach the bank for financing, **your strategy must become more proactive.** The following tips come from a combination of personal experience and interviews with small business bankers and other business owners:

**1) You must be prepared.** Have your business plan ready. Show you have thought about your business and potential financial needs. Make the package presentable and neat. Make sure you include all the documents the bank has requested. Your professional image can be tarnished if they need to make numerous requests for additional information.

**2) Find an advocate for your company in the bank.** You will need someone in the bank willing to go to bat for you and your business. Many times loans fall into the gray area between being approved and denied. With an advocate on your side, your chances of approval are greater.

Make sure the advocate can really help. You do not want to spend time selling a person on your company only to find they have no influence on the approval of your loan. Be clear about what you want and why you believe you should have it.

**3) Be an advocate for yourself.** A banker friend of mine told me, while I was going through one of our first loan requests, " If they tell you no, make them tell you why not. If you don't like that answer, take your case directly to the person in the bank that can change the decision."

**Many times persistence is all that it takes.** Making your case in person is always the best method. I had a banker ask me to drop my business plan and data at the nearest branch office, and it would be forwarded to him. It was important for me to explain that this process was too impersonal for my situation. I told the banker that I did not want my package to be one of many on his desk. With no face or personal contact to set our plan apart, we may not be successful.

We met the next morning and spent 35 minutes reviewing our documentation. I did not tell him this, but I would have gone to another bank rather than send the package to him through the nearest branch office. Paper is easy to refuse, but refusing a person face to face is tougher. Use any advantage you can to make it tough for the bank to say no.

**4) Shop around.** No bank or banker is alike. There are many factors that contribute to the outcome of your loan request: the experience of the loan officer, his understanding of your business, incentive plans or loan sale promotions going on at the time, and even the mood of the particular loan officer.

What if the morning you delivered your loan request, the loan officer was reprimanded for a bad loan that he had written. Do you believe the officer is going to be willing to grant your company a loan? Now is the time to use the bank contacts you have built over time.

Since you have kept in touch (I hope) with all of them, they will be familiar with your business situation. You will get different results from different banks. If they all approve your loan, you get the opportunity to choose the best deal for your business.

Our company went to the bank to restructure some of our short term debt and increase our line of credit. We went to the banker who held our existing line of credit. (We didn't shop around). The bank approved our loan request, but put very limiting requirements on the use of the money. Since we had not applied to any other institution we were stuck. Going to another bank would mean starting over. No other banker knew us. We needed the extended funds, so we were forced to accept terms that we did not like.

The next day we prepared packages for two other banks. We now have personal relationships with three banks. They all know our financial position, company strategy and objectives. You never know when a bank officer will get promoted or leave the bank. If this is the only contact you have, you could be in trouble. Banking is just like every other business: Relationship, relationship, relationship.

**5) Get it before you need it.** It is easiest to get bank financing when your finances are strong. Some experts think you should get a small loan before you really need one. Pay off the loan as agreed. This will establish both a track record and a relationship with the bank. To make this strategy work best for you, remember to make the loan small. You don't want a loan that will hurt your business or personal finances.

The bottom line is that banks are in the business of loaning and being repaid money. Build your bank relationships early. When you make the decision to get bank financing, your challenge is to give the bank as many reasons as possible to say yes. Be prepared, be professional, and be persistent. What you show on paper is important, but the banker must be able to trust you personally.

*18*

# Venture Capital Financing

*"I don't care how many times you hear the word no. You ain't gonna give up. Either live north or die!"*
— Harriet Tubman,
Conductor,
Underground Railroad

*W* hat does the venture capitalist want? Venture capital firms are usually looking for relatively new businesses that have exceptionally high growth potential. It is the high growth and return on investment that will bring the venture capital firm their profit. **An expected return of 3 to 5 times their investment is not unusual**. A company is attractive to a venture capital firm when it meets the following criteria:

1) High but realistic financial projections
2) A clearly unique attribute of your business
3) An experienced and hungry management team
4) A good clear exit strategy for the venture capitalist.

**Venture capital is an equity form of financing.** The term equity means ownership. In this case, equity is ownership in your company. Venture capital companies give businesses money in exchange for a percentage ownership in the business. Venture capital firms often want to own a majority interest in the businesses in which they invest. If your company is a certified minority business enterprise (also referred to as disadvantaged business enterprise (DBE) or historically underutilized business (HUB)), the majority ownership of a non-minority venture capital firm could risk this status. Consult the certifying agency to determine the true impact.

Unlike other financing sources, venture capitalists will pay more attention to the product you sell, your company's position in the market place and your personal ability to manage your company. **It is important to understand the venture capital firm becomes an owner (and often a majority owner) in your company.**

Many times the venture capitalist will want to add or replace important management personnel. They will plan to maintain their investment in your company for five to seven years. Part of any decision for venture capital investment is also a strategy to exit the company at some future date.

**An exit strategy is a plan to withdraw their original investment plus any growth that has occurred over the time they have been a part of your company.** There are various methods for a venture capital firm to exit a business. These topics are advanced and beyond the scope of this book. Consult an accountant or lawyer with experience in this area.

## How Do You Increase Your Chances of Getting Venture Capital?

Venture capital firms receive hundreds and often thousands of business proposals a year. They reject as many as 97% of the proposals they receive, but you can increase your chances of getting a positive response from a venture capital company. Assuming your company meets the basic requirements attractive to a venture capitalist, doing your homework and preparing an exceptional proposal will put you in position to get a favorable response.

Do your homework. Find out a little about the firm you are approaching. Try to get to know an individual from the fund. You will need to know as much as possible about the types of companies in which they invest. Do they focus on a particular industry? What are they looking for in the business proposal? What return on investment are they expecting? Are they focused in a particular geographical area?

You only want to pursue the firms that are interested in your type of business. You should also do your homework on your own business. Your knowledge of your business and your industry will be critical. How your growth rate, profit margin, and return on investment compare to the industry will be one very critical set of numbers to know and understand.

Now that you have done your homework, you are ready to prepare your business proposal. It cannot be mentioned too often that these companies get hundreds of proposals a year. Although they are in the business of investing capital, they have little patience for poorly prepared plans. Use your research information to target areas that you are certain are of interest.

Highlight the four areas mentioned above. The plan should be upbeat and positive without being untruthful. A clear statement of the purpose of the requested funds is a must. An easy to understand marketing strategy will give the reviewers a feel for how you plan to continue to grow the company.

Keep the proposal under fifty pages, and it should be typed. Add color and bind the package if you can. Anything that gets someone to take your proposal seriously will help separate your package from the masses.

Concentrate on the flow of the package. You are telling a

story, and it must make sense and hold the reader's attention. Tie all things to growth and return on investment because these are the things venture capital firms will be looking for. Once you have delivered your proposal, be sure to follow-up. You want to appear to be interested without looking desperate.

Venture capital can be a great source of financing for companies that are growing at a very fast pace. Remember venture capitalists give money in exchange for a percentage of ownership. Know what types of businesses the venture firm wants to finance, and be prepared to sell the total view of your business. The management team, product, customers, and projected performance are all important factors. You will probably only get one chance. Be ready.

*19*

# *Selecting the Right Financing Method*

*"Do unto others as you would have them do unto you."*
—The Golden Rule

S electing the appropriate financing method for your business can be confusing. African-Americans usually think of banks when they think of financing. It has been mentioned before that black business owners still fare poorly when they seek bank financing. Part of the reason for our poor record with banks is that bank financing is often the wrong financing method to use. Most businesses in our community need more equity or investment of money by the owners. Trying to get bank financing with no equity is a long shot. Consider the following five issues as you decide the best way to finance your business.

**1) Cost.** What is the cost of the financing? How high is the interest rate? What is the investor expecting as a return?

**2) Effect on business.** How will the particular financing affect the business? What will the new money do to the balance sheet? Can the business make all payments required?

**3) Flexibility.** How flexible is the financing source? Can

**Figure 19.1. How Are People Financing Start-up Small Businesses**

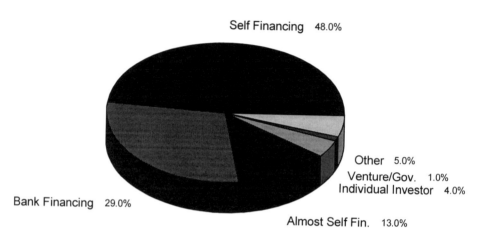

Self Financing   48.0%

Other   5.0%
Venture/Gov.   1.0%
Individual Investor   4.0%

Bank Financing   29.0%

Almost Self Fin.   13.0%

Source: Wall Street Journal 1994

you use the funds for the things you think are best for the business or must the money be used for a specific purpose such as real estate, working capital, or inventory?

**4) Control.** Does the financing affect the control you have of the company? Will you still be able to make the decisions you think are best for your business?

**5) Availability.** Is the financing there and available to you? Can you gain access to the money? Is the structure of your business ready for the desired financing method?

Almost half of all small businesses started in the United States are started using the personal funds of the business owner (Figure 19.1). In contrast, this chart, derived from a *Wall Street Journal* article, shows that less than 1% of all small businesses use venture capital to get started.

You must weigh the five considerations above and determine which are most important to you. **Many times the decision boils down to the fifth consideration, availability.** It would be great if you could select the type of financing you wanted. In the real world, you may be forced to select from the few options you have.

**Do not go after a loan (debt) too soon.** Debt must be paid back with interest. If you take debt, you want it to be based on the performance of the business, not on you personally. This will be difficult to do if you are just starting. If you do choose debt, be sure your business can pay all of its' expenses plus the additional debt service.

**Keep your business as flexible as possible and always keep control.** Never let any investor own more than you do. Consider nontraditional funding. Look to your church or local civic organizations. If your idea is well-planned and well-presented, your community can help you get the money you need. Review the various financing options stated above. Lean toward self-financing when you can. You will have plenty of time to get money from outside sources.

# *Part VI:*
# *Structuring Your Business*

There are a few other items that you should consider as you complete the structure of your business. Issues such as proper business planning, selecting a solid technical support team, picking the right company name, choosing a business structure, and identifying needed paperwork will all be important if you plan to succeed in business.

20

---

# Developing Your Business Plan

*"It's pretty hard for the Lord to guide you if you haven't made up your mind which way you want to go."*
    —Madame C.J. Walker
        Entrepreneur & Philanthropist

*A* business plan is a document that describes your business in detail. The business plan is the business in paper form. It includes what you are selling, how you will sell it, who you will sell it to, how you will finance the company, and who will manage the business. The business plan should be prepared early and revisited and revised often.

There are three major reasons for having a business plan. **First, the plan will test your business idea before you get started.** The business plan is a business simulation tool. Without investing any money your plan will tell you if your idea has a chance of success. It will help you to answer simple questions such as: Are there enough people in your area to support your new business? Since few of us have money to waste, it is best we answer all the questions about our potential business before we invest our money.

A second reason to have a business plan is that it can be used as a unifying tool for partners and associates. Your business plan is a central tool that you can use to make sure that every person involved with your business has a good understanding of the strategy and projections of the company. Periodic review of the business plan will help you make decisions consistent with your stated business objectives. The plan is your business rallying point. Effectively used it can motivate, focus, and guide your business resources.

The third reason for having a business plan is that it provides valuable information for banks and potential investors. A good business plan will make bankers more knowledgeable about your business. The time when you need financing is the wrong time to prepare your business plan. You should always have an up-to-date business plan ready. Private investors will want to read your plan to better understand where their investment is going and how you plan to provide an acceptable financial return.

For all the things a business plan can do for your business, it should not be your excuse for not getting started. My sister recently had her third child. She and her husband decided she would quit working and stay home with my nieces, who are all under the age of four. After being home for a few months, she felt the need to contribute to the finances of the household, but she did not want to leave the children in daycare all day.

A natural fit was for her to start her own daycare center. She called me with questions about how she should go about writing her business plan. She began researching locations, education curriculums, and funding sources. The plan required much more time and effort than she had anticipated.

During one of our many telephone conversations, I suggested that she get started on a smaller scale as she continued to build her plan for a major daycare center. Before long she began taking care of one additional child, then two, and so on. She not only brought in enough money to help with home expenses, but his quick start helped to keep her motivated as she continued to build her business plan. This get-started-quick option is not for everyone and every business. You must be committed to completing your business plan or your business future will be limited.

At the same time, you do not want to spend too long developing your plan. Set a date when the plan will be completed and work everyday toward that goal. Do not sweat the details. The plan is important; but as one of my business partners always says, "You're not building a watch. It doesn't have to be that exact."

A dollar here or there is not going to change the effectiveness of your plan. If you can't find a piece of data, make a note of it and move on. You need a plan before you get started, but don't let the development of the plan stop you. If you are struggling with the numbers, skip them and move on to the parts that come more easily for you. Get some help and come back to the numbers later.

The key is to commit to working on your plan everyday. Get it done. There is strength with momentum, and you need to get your business momentum started early. The momentum will become contagious, and your company will grow at an exponential rate.

Use the Business Plan Primer in Appendix A of this book. It will give you an outline of the business plan structure as well as provide you with examples on the words to use in each section.

_____

## 21

# Selecting Your Technical Support Team

*"Don't ask for anyone's advice unless you are prepared to use it."*
—Sammy Davis, Jr. Entertainer

*T*hroughout the time you spend building your business, you will rely on the expertise of various professionals. Your need for them will vary based on the particular skills that you already have. Identify an attorney, accountant, banker, and small business consultant very early in the planning process of your company. These four major sources of technical support will be important resources for your business. This chapter gives you tips on selecting the support professional best for your business.

## Accountant and Attorney

Your attorney and accountant can be selected in pretty much the same way. You should look for three significant traits. First, and most important, is a general feeling of comfort with both the attorney and accountant. Do they listen to you until they thoroughly understand your situation? Do they return your telephone calls in a timely fashion? Do you trust the advice they give? You should consider this a long-term relationship because you will have to invest time and effort into giving them the information that they need to really understand your business. Changing your accountant or attorney later could be costly to you.

Second, check the experience of the professional. Do they have experience with your type of business? Are they familiar with small companies? Check references and ask any questions that you may have. This person is going to work for you. If they don't want to answer your questions and provide you with references, move on. They are not the professional for your business.

The last thing to consider is how much these professionals charge. You never want to pay too much, but paying too little can also be dangerous. If either of these two individuals makes just one mistake, you could be out of business. Find someone who has reasonable rates. Consider three or four firms and compare their charges. Ask them what you can do yourself to hold down the cost. Try to find accountants and attorneys who will charge a flat fee for a particular project. You want to know all your costs before the work is done.

## Banker and Business Consultant

You should select a banker as early as possible. The earlier you establish a relationship with a banker, the better your chances will be when you really need money. Read chapter 17 to get more information on building your banking relationship. It is a good idea to put yourself in the place of the banker. Would you talk to someone for twenty minutes and give them thousands of dollars based on what they told you? Of course you wouldn't.

Bankers feel better when they have a relationship with you. Then if everything is not perfect in your application, the banker will consider your relationship and will be more liekely to assist you in approving the loan. Remember relationships are important. Look for a banker who is interested in hearing about your business.

Talk to other business owners about the lenders with the best reputation dealing with African-American businesses. Relying totally on the opinions of others is never good, but the more input you have, the better your banking decision will be.

A business consultant is the final person that you need for your technical support team. Everyone will not need a business consultant. However, if you have many questions about how the basics of business work, a business consultant may be a good idea.

A business consultant can help you with marketing strategy, business planning, and a variety of other general business subjects. If you need this kind of assistance, help is available. A good place to look for a small business consultant is local minority business support organizations. Groups like minority supplier development councils, minority business incubators, and even state development organizations often supply technical support at low or no rates. Do not forget to check with organizations like the Senior Corps Of Retired Executives (SCORE) and the Small Business Administration (SBA) .

There are many programs directed at helping minority businesses with technical support (Consult Appendix B of this book). Many of these organizations can also provide assistance with accounting and legal issues. Other business owners can be a good source for finding competent technical assistance. Ask established business owners who they use.

Selecting the proper technical support team takes time, effort, and perhaps some trial and error. Start early, ask a lot of questions, and remember these people will be working for you.

22

---

# Picking the Right Company Name

*"Wisdom is the principal thing; therefore get wisdom and with all thy getting get understanding."*

—Proverbs 4:7

*T*he selection of a company name is more important than most business owners realize. We spend long hours planning to go into business and then select a business name without much thought at all. Your business name identifies your company and establishes your business image.

A business name often gives an indication of the type of company you are running and why someone should want to use your service or buy your product. Including words like economical, value, best, quality, and rapid in your company name will tell your potential client a great deal about your business.

Future plans are important when you are selecting a company name. Will you want to provide other products or services in the future? Will your company name still work for these new business areas? If you name your company Auto

Transmission Incorporated and you later want to repair mufflers, the name may hurt your expansion plans. You cannot know everything you may want to do in the future, but don't select a name without at least thinking about what changes you might want to make later.

African-American businesses often use names that denote their ethnic heritage. Names like Ebony Services or Ujima Paper Products tells everyone that your company is minority owned. If the fact that your business is owned by blacks is important to the operation of your business, then an ethnic name is a good idea. Stay away from ethnic names unless it adds value to your business. If the ethnic name is not bringing in business, you don't want it to keep business away.

Some individuals, from all ethnic groups, will not do business with African American companies. There are many reasons for their position (See chapter 28 for more information on the Minority Business Enterprises). If your name reveals that your company is black-owned, you may never get the chance to demonstrate that you can provide quality products or services. Staying away from ethnic names has nothing to do with being ashamed of your heritage and everything to do with business. Select the name that is best for your business.

A company name that consists of your personal name is fine if this practice is common in your particular business environment. Law practices, accounting firms, consultants, and architects are all businesses where it is common to use your name as the company name. Some people use their name and add the term & Associates. (i.e. Johnson & Associates). Although this practice is common in certain businesses, it is not a must. Always consider other options.

Other types of businesses rarely use the owner's name as the company name. Businesses such as manufacturing, distribution, and computer companies may appear like small time players if the company name is the same as the owners name. Think about how a business card would look if it read Smith Distribution, Roberta Smith, President. The person reading the card may assume that Roberta Smith is the only person in the company. If the business card reads West Coast Distribution, Roberta Smith, President, the company appears to be larger and more established.

Consider many names before you settle on one. List the names on paper and run them by others for their input. Ask others what they think of when they see or hear the name.

Once you select a company name, it will be difficult and expensive to change it. Be sure the name you choose is the one you want. Before you make your final selection, check with your state and/or local government to be sure the name is not already being used. Read chapter 24 for more information on certifying your business name.

# 23

# Deciding on a Business Structure

*....for when I am weak, then am I strong.*
                    —II Corinthians 12:10

*B*usiness structure is the **official business form** of your enterprise. You will have many options when it comes to selecting a structure. Read this section to determine which structure sounds best for your situation. If you still have questions, contact your attorney for professional assistance.

When considering business structure, your first decision should be whether your company will be a "for-profit" or a "not-for-profit" (non-profit) business. Don't be too quick to choose the for-profit structure. There are many major benefits to being a non-profit company. Depending on your type of business, non-profit status may even be more desirable.

## Non-Profit Company

There are three major advantages to being a not-for-profit business:

**1) A non-profit company can receive charitable gifts from**

other companies, government agencies, and individuals. These funds could change your charitable passion into a viable business.

**2) Revenue in excess of cost is not taxable.** (Revenue is all the money your company brings in. Cost is everything you pay out.) In addition, you do not have to pay sales tax on your company purchases.

**3) Incorporating a non-profit company is a fairly simple process.** You can probably file the papers yourself. This will save you the cost of attorney fees.

You should also understand and consider the **disadvantages** of being a non-profit company:

**1) A non-profit corporation must have an active board of directors.** The company is actually owned by the directors, and they ultimately have complete control of the company. This takes much of the control from you, the founder of the enterprise. Although it rarely happens, the board could even vote to remove you from your job as the head of the company.

**2) There are no profits from a non-profit company.** All revenues in excess of cost must be used to further the stated mission of the non-profit company. Your compensation comes from a set salary approved by the board.

## *For-Profit Enterprises*

We are all more familiar with business enterprises that are operated to make a profit. The advantages of a non-profit are, for the most part, the disadvantages of a for-profit business. Simply stated a for-profit business is one whose owners can pocket the excess of revenue over expenditures (cost).

There are three key advantages to being a for-profit company:

**1) The owners control the company.** Although a board of directors may be needed, the owners decide on the board members. The company is owned by the owners.
**2) The owners can take the profits of the company as personal income.**
**3) There are no limits as to the type of business that you can conduct.** The business need only be legal.

There are three major disadvantages of being a for-profit enterprise:
1) For-profit companies must pay taxes on profits.
**2) Some owners of profit companies may have to pay company taxes on profits to the business and personal taxes for profits distributed to the owners.** This is known as double taxation.
**3) The paper work for incorporating some for-profit companies can be complex to prepare and expensive to file.**

There are other disadvantages that pertain to particular types of for-profit business structures. You should understand the various forms of profit companies.
   **Sole proprietorships.** The sole proprietorship is the simplest form of business structure. The advantages are ease of formation, reduced expenses, and total control. The owner is recipient of all profits and the business is easy to terminate.
   A sole proprietorship means one owner. You are the company. The disadvantage is that some people will not do business with companies who are not incorporated. Since you and the company are one, the liabilities of the business become your personal liabilities. All debt, suits, and liens will be your personal responsibility.
   Another disadvantage to a sole proprietorship is that the business ends when the owner dies. You cannot pass a sole proprietorship on to the next generation.

**Partnerships.** Partnerships are also a very popular form of business structure. Information about creating effective partnerships is covered in Chapter 25. A partnership is a lot like a sole proprietorship. The difference is that the business ownership is shared between two or more individuals.

Starting a partnership is more complex than establishing a sole proprietorship. A document should be written (I would suggest by an attorney) that outlines each partner's percentage of ownership in the company as well as how any profits or losses will be distributed. The document should also specify how decisions will be made among the partners and what happens upon the death or separation of any partner. Much like a sole proprietorship, partners are personally liable for the actions of the business enterprise.

**Corporations.** Corporations are the most complex of all the business structures. The cost and complexity of establishing your business as a corporation can be significant. The tax implications of some corporate structures can also be a major disadvantage.

The major advantage is that a corporation becomes an entity unto itself. The company continues to live with or without the original owners. Many people like the structure of the corporation because it can limit the personal liability of the owners.

Two major forms of corporations are the sub-chapter S corporation and the general corporation. The sub-chapter S corporation looks a lot like a partnership or sole proprietorship. Taxes are paid at the individual level just as in a partnership or sole proprietorship.

Sub-chapter S corporations must have a board of directors. You can enjoy the benefit of the protection of being a corporation and avoid the double taxation and much of the complexity that comes with incorporating. Sub-chapter S corporations are very popular with small business owners. The volume of paper work increases compared to the levels for partnerships and sole proprietorships but is still much less than for a general corporation.

The general corporation is the business form of most large companies in the United States. Corporations must have a board of directors. A major disadvantage to the corporate structure is something called double taxation. The corporation is taxed as its own entity. Then the owners are taxed when they receive their share of the corporate profits. Since the same dollars are taxed twice, it is called double taxation. The corporate entity continues even in the event of the illness or death of the owner.

## How Do You Decide Which Structure Is Best for Your Business?

Your decision about business structure should not be taken lightly. Rely on your technical support team (see Chapter 21 for details on the technical support team you will need) for expert advice. But you now have a basic understanding of the different business structures. As you consider the various business structures, use the following criteria to guide your thought process. You must weigh these factors to determine which are most important to you and your business:

**1) Cost** - Can you afford the cost to establish the business structure? Have you considered the tax ramifications?

**2) Value** - Do you need the skills, talents, and resources of others as owners in your business?

**3) Organizational flexibility** - Do you feel a need for a board of directors? Do you mind establishing officers and structured positions?

**4) Stability** - How stable will your business be during illness or when you want to take time off?

Is the continuance of your business during illness or death

**Figure 23.1. Selecting the Best Business Structure**

> **Factors impacting your decision on best structure**
>     1) Cost
>     2) The Value of Partners
>     3) Organizational Flexibility
>     4) Continuity of Business
>     5) Associated Risk
>     6) Taxation Implications
>     7) The Influence of Laws (federal, local, and state)
>
>     8) External Factors (Customers, etc.)

important to you?

**5) Risk** - What are the risks associated with each type of organizational structure? Are you concerned about business liability?

**6) Taxation** - Is the double taxation of the corporate structure acceptable to you?

**7) Laws** (federal, local, and state) - Do certain laws mandate your business to be a particular business structure?

**8) Factors unique to your business** - Will your potential customers demand a particular business structure?

Your business is unique, and the business structure you select should be the best for your needs. Keep your business objectives in mind. Your advisors (lawyer and accountant) can give you expert advice. Ask these experts about the pros and cons for your particular business and individual situation. Although the experts can give you advice, only you should make the final decision.

## *Do You Really Want to Do It Yourself?*

Many business owners want to personally prepare the

paperwork to establish their business structure. Doing the work yourself will save you money, but depending on the type of business structure you choose, it can be a very complex process. If you choose a sole proprietorship, there is very little you must do. Simply contact the appropriate state office (usually the Attorney General's office) and inquire about the needed paper work.

If you decide on a partnership, the issue is slightly more complex. I always suggest that you use a lawyer to document the relationship between the partners. Items such as what happens upon the death of one of the partners, how profits will be distributed, and what happens if one of the partners wants to get out of the business are issues best addressed by an attorney. If you insist on doing it yourself, standard partnership agreements can be found in the library or a local bookstore.

Incorporating a business that is non-profit or has only one owner is fairly simple. You can purchase incorporation kits at your local bookstore. If your business is a corporation with more than one stock holder or other special considerations, you may want to take your case to an attorney.

Getting this process done correctly will help you avoid problems in the future. There are many how-to books in the library. Some of the more complex structures should be approached with caution. It is possible to do the proper filings yourself, but you have to be sure that you understand the process.

There are pros and cons to all of the business structures outlined in this chapter. Choosing a business structure is an important decision, but completing this step should not prevent you from moving forward. You can always incorporate your sole proprietorship or partnership later. Continue to review your business structure as your business grows. Change the structure when and if it makes sense to do so.

24
_____

# Business Certification, License, and Insurance

*"Get it done in the beginning so you'll be ready when the time comes."*

—Brad Lightfoot
Partner, Infrastructure Services, Inc.


*W* hile you are completing paperwork, check with your state and local governments to determine the requirements for doing business in your location. You will probably need to at least file for regiestration of a fictitious name. This is a simple form telling the state that your enterprise is doing business under your chosen business name.

Contact the business development office of your local government and the state office of business development for leads to the proper agencies. Be prepared to see a lot of paperwork. The list of forms seems overwhelming, but many of the forms may not be related to your business.

Paperwork alone has stopped many businesses from ever getting started. Starting simple will reduce the amount of paperwork that you will be required to complete. Consider starting as a sole proprietorship. As your needs grow, you can always enter a more complex business structure. It is important to complete the vital items and leave the others for later. The objective is to get yourself in business as quickly as possible.

In addition to general business paperwork, your particular business may have its own set of needed licenses, certifications, and insurance. Do your research early to avoid being surprised. Call local support groups and associations in your industry and ask what is needed.

Customers sometimes require you to have a certain level of liability insurance. Check with your potential clients to determine their requirements. Some types of business liability insurance can be very expensive. Shop around as always and never buy a dollar more than you need. Always wait until the day you need it to buy more.

You can decide to make your company a certified minority business enterprise (MBE). Some people refer to them as historically underutilized businesses (HUBs) or disadvantaged business enterprises (DBEs). This is a certification given to businesses owned and operated by individuals from qualified minority groups. If you decide to qualify your business for certification under one of these programs, there will be other sets of documents that you will need to complete.

Find out who the important certifying agencies are for your type of business. Getting certified with one agency rarely means you are certified with others. A good starting point is certification with your local government and other major cities in the area. Consider getting your MBE status with the state in which you are located.

The last major certifying body is your local chapter of the National Minority Supplier Development Council. Certification with this organization will improve your access to private corporations in your area. Since this group has a national affiliation, you will be able to get certified in other cities that have chapters of the national minority supplier development group.

The last area in this section is probably the most important. If you are leaving your job to run your company full-time, **make sure you have your health insurance in place**. Don't wait until you quit your job to go after health insurance. The rules on who will be insured and who won't are changing everyday. Shop around for the best price. But try your best to have health insurance at all times.

# Part VII:
# Considering Other Factors

This section is full of miscellaneous concepts and ideas that could mean the difference between your success and failure in business. Included are helpful tips on running a part-time business, taking advantage of technology, and selecting a partner. Also included are issues related to being certified as a minority business enterprise (MBE).

25

# Do You Really Need a Partner?

*Confidence in an unfaithful man in time of trouble is like a broken tooth, and a foot out of joint.*

—Proverbs 25:19

*D*etermining your need for a business partner can be a puzzling issue. It is tempting to want to have someone to share the ups and downs with you. The African-American business owners that I interviewed talked about the security of going into business with a partner.

African-Americans starting a business know that they will have to endure many trials in order to grow their business to any level of success. By adding a partner, the new business owner gains the confidence to take on the challenges of growing a business.

Entrepreneurs who have been in business for a while have a different perspective. Business owners who once had partners point to the horror stories related to business partnerships. A successful owner of a medical equipment company says he had two partners when he started his business almost ten years ago. This business owner says it only took a few months to realize the threesome was not working out:

"It was difficult to get everyone working at the same level. My partners were not carrying their weight."

**The most common reason for the failure of business partnerships is this difficulty in putting together the right skill levels to properly divide the workload.** One partner often feels overburdened if they are doing the bulk of the work. Finding the perfect mix of talent to spread the work load evenly is next to impossible.

Partners are usually picked based on relationships that have already formed. We look to friends, relatives, church members, or fraternity brothers for business partners. None of these characteristics are good reasons to select someone to go into business with you.

Business partnerships fair little better than marriages. Studies show that 50% of all business partnerships fail. If you feel that you need a partner in your business, you need to understand the factors that can increase your chances of maintaining a long-term partnership.

## Why Should You Consider Having a Partner?

**Consider a business partner if you and your business are lacking something that you are sure you are going to need and can get no other way.** For example, many people ask how I got into the engineering business since nothing in my background gives me any engineering experience. The answer is simple. My partner and I saw the value of each other's talents.

He is an outstanding civil and structural engineer. When we started our business, he had more than ten years of experience in the engineering consulting industry. By adding my marketing and business background we had a complete business. Our roles were clear. It was my job to get business, his job was to perform the services, and my job was to be sure that we got paid for the work our company had performed.

Even with our roles clearly defined, there are times when issues of workload and responsibility cause problems. Just as in a marriage we must continue to communicate our frustrations in a clear and mature fashion. With this communication, we have built a successful business.

Equal workloads in a partnership may not be possible. Instead of looking for equal workload, you should look for equal commitment to the business. Business partnerships can work and be very rewarding. There are four things you can do to increase your chances of developing a thriving business partnership (Figure 25.1):

**Figure 25.1. Surviving a Business Partnership**

**Four Secrets of Surviving Partnerships**

1.) Make sure you *really* need a partner.
2.) Make sure your partner has the skills they say they have.
3.) Be sure the objectives and expectations are known and written before you start.
4.) Keep the lines of communication open.

**1.) Make sure you need a partner.** The partner(s) should fill a needed gap in your business, and he must make the business better. The person must add value.

**2.) Make sure your partner has the skills that she claims to have.** Many times business owners select someone because they like them and believe they have potential. You need a partner who has the skills now.

**3.) Be sure the business objectives and expectations are known and written before you get started.** You must have common financial, spiritual, ethical, and work expectations. Put all of your objectives in writing, so there is no room for misunderstanding. A business plan, understood and agreed to by all partners, will help make sure everyone is on the same page.

**4) Keep the lines of communication open.** Communication in a partnership is as important as in a marriage. You and your partners must be able to honestly talk about feelings, frustrations and ideas. Open communication will keep all the partners in sync and avoid problems in the future.

Forming a partnership for any other reason than a real need for something in the business is rarely a good idea. Do not add partners because of their race, sex, or your need for companionship. Most African-American business owners are agree that in the long-run it is better to be in business on your own. Partnerships can work, but like a marriage, they take a great deal of work to maintain. Make sure your effort is worth it.

26
_____

# Your Part-time Business and Your Full-time Job

*"People ask me how I built my business. I tell them 'I didn't have much, but I used everything I had.'"*
—Thomas Burrell
Founder
Burrell Communications

*P* eople often minimize the importance of part-time businesses. Any level of additional income can make a significant difference in the way you live. For example, imagine your life with as little as $8,000 extra a year in income. That is $667 more a month to spend as you please. Would you live in a different house, give more to your favorite charity, drive a nicer car or simply be able to save more money for your children's college education?

The point is you could live differently. Part-time businesses can make a difference. You should not wait to start your business because you have a full-time job. Whether you plan to one day leave your job and become a full-time business owner or operate your business part-time forever, both methods can work. The key is to get started.

Most small and minority entrepreneurs start their business ventures while working a full-time job. The long hours and additional stress of running a part-time business often drive the new entrepreneur to give up on the dream well before they have a chance to be successful.

Running a part-time business requires more effort, but the rewards can be significant. Successfully managing both your full-time job and your part-time business is possible. Some business owners run successful part-time businesses for years and realize great rewards.

Connie Rudolph of Connie's Collectibles makes and sells African-American collectable dolls from her home part-time. She works full-time for a large consumer products company. What is her secret to holding it all together? Connie says "You must be extremely organized."

Your effective use of time and money will be vital as you attempt to do the things needed to succeed as a part-time business owner. If you have little time, you will need to spend money in some form to get others to do the work your company needs done. If you have little money, then you will have to spend time performing your business activities personally.

There are creative ways to get others motivated to help your business grow. Just keep in mind, no matter what your particular situation, every business decision you make will be in some way related to your use of either time, money, or both.

Here are four basic tips for success in starting your part-time business:

**1) Make the commitment.** Ask yourself if you really want to put the effort into owning your own business and still work a full-time job. Along with the many rewards of business ownership there are many issues that will test your level of commitment to your new enterprise. Make sure you and

**Figure 26.1. Your Entrepreneurial Resources**

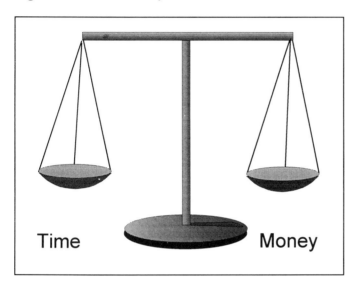

Time             Money

your family understand the time and effort it will take to be successful. If you don't know what your new venture will take, ask other part-time entrepreneurs. Ms. Rudolph says, "It is a job! You must commit to it just like any other job." It is no coincidence that I mention commitment first. As an entrepreneur, you must be totally committed to the success of the business.

**2) Leverage your resources.** Your biggest obstacle to success will be your limited amount of resources. Leverage means using tools to make your valuable resources do more. As a part-time entrepreneur, your most important resources are time and money. Since you work a job, you will probably be short on time.

You can leverage your limited time by developing partnerships or contracts with people to handle things that you don't have time to do. Find an independent salesperson or broker to sell your product while you are working. Arrange to pay on a commission basis to preserve limited money.

This method will cost you little until your product is actually sold.

You may also consider selling your product through retail shops. Many shops will sell your product for a share of the profits. Since retailers only make money when the product is sold, they will be motivated to sell your product. This method is often called selling on consignment.

You may even consider using other independent business owners to perform many of the task of your business. Find business owners whose skills you trust, and hire them to do the things that you do not have the time to do. Set up your business to allow for the use of the time and money of others. You will have to give up part of your profit to pay for it, but your business will have an opportunity to grow while you continue to work full-time.

**3) Get the right tools.** Make the investment in putting yourself in business. Get business letterhead and cards printed. Install a separate telephone line in your home (if you are working from your home and can afford the extra expense).

Purchase a reliable answering machine or use your local telephone company's voice message system. You must be able to get your messages and return your calls. Buy or lease a computer and a quality printer (See chapter 27 for information on using technology in your business). Also consider installing a basic fax machine. The fax has become a piece of equipment every business is assumed to have.

These items will cost you money, but without them, your long-term prospects for success are low. Buy the most important items first. As your business brings in revenue, continue to invest in the other items your business will need. These items will give you the right tools to effectively run a part-time business.

**4) Use your tools.** Investing in the proper business tools is only part of the challenge of running a part-time business. The most important prerequisite for success in a part-time business is to use your tools to maintain a high level of professionalism. It is not what you have, but what you do with what you have that counts. If your part-time business appears to be a sideline business to your potential customers, many will shy away from doing business with you.

For example, if a client calls you and leaves a message and does not receive a call back, they can only assume you are not serious about your business. Following a simple rule will solve this problem: Do what you say you are going to do, when you say you are going to do it.

Remember, no client or customer cares that you have a full-time job, kids or many social responsibilities. Your customers want service. They will either get it from you or from someone else. Check your messages at lunch time and return all calls. If your employer will allow it, take your lunch either before noon or after one o'clock Your chances of finding your client in their office will increase, and the fact that you run a part-time business will be less of an issue.

Running a business part-time can work if you commit yourself to the success. Never make excuses for not getting things done. Your customers will not mind you working a full-time job unless you let your job impact your business' performance. Tell your clients what you can do and always deliver on your promises. Your business will grow to whatever level you desire.

*27*

---

# *Taking Advantage of Technology*

*"It would be foolish to expect to chop down an oak tree with a pocket knife."*

—Melvin J. Gravely, Sr.

*M*ost African-American business owners start small businesses. Rarely do we bring in millions of dollars in investments to begin our operations. We typically have few employees, little money, and limited, if any, office space. Most of the businesses started by African-Americans are part-time businesses. The way that we start our businesses is often a reason for the way the business is perceived by the public.

Few customers want to do business with a company that appears to be a start-up or a part-time business. With the declining cost of technology, there is no excuse for your business not appearing to be  professional.

The first tier or the basic technology of a beginning business is a telephone and a reliable answering machine. Your customers must have a consistent method of reaching you. Your telephone number can be the same as your home telephone, but I suggest that you get another number from the beginning upfront. This will avoid the need to possibly change your business number later. Your answering machine must be one you can count on. If you are planning to buy a new machine, shop around for the best deal. Answering machines with separate tapes for your recorded message and the incoming message will last longer.

Another answering system option is to purchase this service from your local telephone company. The advantage of this option is your messages will be recorded even if you are already on the telephone. Your customers will never get a busy signal and you will always get their message. This service should cost under $10 per month in addition to your current local telephone charges.

As your business grows and your level of activity increases, you will need to invest the second tier of business technology. A fax machine and personal computer (PC) will help your company be more competitive and appear more professional. There are many choices when considering a fax machine. Prices can vary from $280 to over $1000. Do your research on the features that you think you will need. Be sure to ask questions about warranty, replacement paper costs, and advantages and disadvantages of each system.

One feature that could be important is the ability of the fax to determine whether the incoming call is a fax or a telephone call. Fax machines with this feature will direct telephone calls to your answering machine and fax transmissions through the fax machine. This will allow you to use one telephone line for both your fax and your telephone calls.

Selecting a personal computer will be your next technology decision. The options are endless, and the technology continues to change quickly. In this section, I'll give you some basic guidelines to use in selecting the best system for your needs. You should then consult your local PC stores for more detail. The first step in selecting a computer system is to know what you will want the system to do. Common requirements are word processing, accounting and desktop publishing. If your business has some other particular need you will want to include it in your list of requirements.

You also want to consider what you could want to do in the future. With today's computer technology your best bet is to buy what you need now and be sure you have the ability to expand your system as your needs change and grow. You should expect to spend between $1,200 and $3,500 for your computer hardware. Software prices vary too greatly to give an accurate range.

Your list of requirements will help you to determine what software you will need. The computer's software tells the computer hardware what to do. Find the software that best meets the needs of your business. Ask others in your business area what software they use. The software you select will dictate what hardware you should purchase.

All software packages list the computer hardware requirements needed to run their package. Add the different software package requirements together to come up with your computer system needs. It is a safe practice to at least triple and preferably quadruple your harddisk requirements to cover for growth and working files. A minimum of four megabytes of main memory is recommended for any new system.

When you are shopping for a computer, be ready to shop around. Prices and deals can vary considerably. There are also mail order computer companies. I do not suggest this option unless you have some experience with PC's or electronics. I also recommend that you stay with the name brands.

Companies like IBM, Compaq, and Apple will give you competitive prices, strong warranties, and good support. Buying a new computer system could literally take forever. Searching through endless software choices, hardware options and company names could give you a case of extreme confusion. Keep you objectives clear and always keep your list of needs in front of you. Set a deadline for when you will make your decision and stick to it.

The third tier of business technology includes the optional accessories you may never need. Items such as copiers, beepers, and cellular telephones. If these items will add to your business performance (and you can afford them), then you should consider adding this technology to your business. Be careful to avoid letting your ego guide your decisions. Only buy the things your business needs and you can afford.

Although the price of most of this technology has come down, you still may not be able to afford it. Don't give up on your business's chances to receive the identified benefits. Copy centers are in the business of providing technology to people who need it and cannot afford to purchase it. One of our engineering offices still does not have a copy machine. The requirements for copying in that office are limited, and it is much cheaper to have our copying performed by a copy center.

Many of these copy centers will let you use the technology at their location, perform the work for you, or rent you the equipment for use at your location. Use your telephone book to find the right mix of location, technology, and price to fit your needs. Your customer will never know you borrowed your technology. The bottom line is that you must use technology to be competitive. If you cannot buy it, then lease it. If you cannot lease it, borrow it.

## *28*

# *The Minority Business Enterprise (MBE)*

*"Sooner or later we've got to polish ourselves up, we've got to let the shine come through."*

—Lou Rawls,
Singer

*T*he term minority business enterprise (MBE) has been used throughout this book. Other titles are disadvantaged businesses enterprise (DBE) or historically underutilized businesses (HUBs). These terms refer to businesses owned and operated by African-Americans, Native-Americans, Hispanic-Americans, and Asian-Americans. This list can vary slightly for different agencies. Some agencies have different terms for each minority group.

For example, in Miami, the term for black-owned businesses is black business enterprise (BBE). These titles were developed in an attempt to identify businesses where a majority of the ownership and control are held by a person or persons from a classified minority group. You will see these terms used as they relate to special programs geared to assisting the population of minority business owners.

A multitude of special programs and years and years of disappointment and frustration have caused many African-American business owners to develop a short-term view of business. Many government agencies and independent consultants have studied the reasons for the high failure rate of minority businesses, and most of these studies have pointed to the same major reasons.

African-American businesses suffer from a lack of access to money, markets, and technical assistance. Research conducted in preparation of this book reveals two additional hurdles blocking the success of minority businesses. **Many minority business owners suffer from a poor image and a misled mind-set about business.** Understanding these issues will help you avoid the pitfalls that have plagued our community for so many years. Developing a plan to survive and even thrive with the help of special programs is critical.

## *Image*

Minority businesses have image problems in both majority and minority communities. The majority community views the minority business as having poorer quality, being undependable and unresponsive, and having higher prices. They have developed this opinion based on their limited exposure to minority businesses and the horror stories passed on to them by friends and business associates.

This community is unforgiving to minority businesses as a population. Once they have had a negative experience, their view is often ruined forever. One bad experience with a minority company means all minority companies are poor performers. Yet when a majority company performs poorly, it is viewed as an isolated incident. This double standard is quite prevalent.

Another reason the majority community has a poor image of black businesses has to do with affirmative action, equal opportunity, and set-aside programs. Over the years, these programs have forced individuals to do business with minorities. When people are forced to do something, they often rebel. These programs make some people think MBE firms are not competitive so they need special programs to get business. All of these thoughts hurt the image of black businesses in the white community.

Black folks are not much better in their treatment of African-American businesses. They suffer from the same view as the majority community. We believe ourselves to be undependable, over priced, and unresponsive. Add these perceptions to a bit of jealousy, and you end up with black businesses not being used and promoted by their own community.

## Misled Mind-set

A self-inflicted inhibitor to minority business success is the issue that bothers me most. The misled mind-set is a dependence on minority set-aside programs for the success of a business. Many blacks start businesses for the sole purpose of taking advantage of the minority set-aside opportunities. Those with this short-term view believe the government and large companies owe us something.

Since minority firms are guaranteed a certain percentage of business, some black business owners pay little attention to the important components of quality products, on-time delivery, and customer service. This attitude continues to feed the poor image problem mentioned above.

Some minority businesses only go after minority set-aside projects. Using this strategy limits your business to the amount of set-asides you can get. It also ensures that you will always be competing against other minority companies. Set-aside projects are meant to be used to gain access to the market-place—to give your company the opportunity to display its skills. These kinds of  programs also allow you to get revenue during the early stages of your business. This early business will get you started on a solid foundation and will make your company more competitive. It is a stretch to call set-asides welfare, but like welfare, the program is not intended to be used as a crutch forever.

Set-aside programs have given some minority business people the idea that they can charge outrageous prices,  provide sub-par services, and still expect more work. If being an MBE gets you access to new markets, special loans, or low-cost office space, it is an advantage. However, the fact that your company is a MBE company means nothing to the average customer. Your customers want to know if your product fits,  you deliver on time, and your price is competitive.

## Access

Access is the most discussed issue effecting the success of black businesses. **Access to three important business ingredients is important: Access to money or capital to start and grow the business, access to markets so that the products or services of a minority business can be sold, and access to technical assistance to assist the minority business owner with financial, management, and marketing issues.**

Minority business owners fail more often than others in their pursuit of the money needed  for their business. The stated reasons are lack of collateral, poor credit history, lack of business experience, and poor or no business plans. In Chapter 17, we discussed what the bank wants from the business owner. Blacks do not often come from a long line of family members with great accumulated wealth. Bankers often have built in bias against black customers. Since the banker rarely understands our situation, we are turned down for loans more often. We cannot use our personal contacts in the banking industry because they still rarely exist.

Without capital it is tough to really grow your business. Many determined African-Americans start without the needed funds. We struggle from day-to-day for many years. Some African-American business owners go after projects larger than their financial position can handle and due to their lack of capital, cannot fulfill their commitments. They blow the project and  become one of the minority businesses that is unresponsive and undependable. Access to capital is a major issue but so is access to markets.

Access to markets is having the opportunity to compete for any business that is available in a given market. Theoretically there is free access to markets. Anyone can pick up the telephone and call anyone else and attempt to market their product or services. The reality is your odds of success are extremely low if you do not know someone in the organization or have a very unique product.

People buy from who they know first, who looks like them second, and who they are not threatened by last. In most cases, we do not know many people in the organization (especially not in positions to influence decisions). We typically do not look like the person making the decision.

Our only hope is to get to the decision maker and convince them, solely on the merits of our product, to do business with our companies. Success in this marketing environment is rare. I always tell the associates in our company, "If no one wants you to win, you probably won't."

Many set-aside programs have hurt the very issue they were meant to help. Set-asides tell the majority community that they must give minorities a certain percentage of the business. No one likes to be told what they must do. In response many in the majority community give the exact percent spelled out in the law and not one percent more. There have been cases where minority companies have been pulled from contracts prior to their completion because the majority company had met the percentage required for the minority set-aside. Some believe the set-aside amount is the maximum amount of business that the minority company is allowed to do. However, the opposite is true; the set-aside percent is the minimum amount of business that the minority company must be given.

Set-aside programs also pit one minority firm against another which which can make for a messy, competitive situation. We spend time wearing each other down instead of going after other business. When I see this happening, it makes me think of slavery days when slaves had limited food to eat and many people to feed. This set-up drives the feeling in our community that in order for one person to win, someone else must lose. It is a dangerous practice, and it is hurting our businesses, our business image, and our community.

Finally, most African-American business owners do not have access to the technical assistance needed to set up and run their business properly. Because of limited funds, we cannot afford expensive consultants, lawyers, and accountants. Since many of our business owners were trained to get jobs and not to provide them, we have few role models that we can go to for assistance. The few we have are working so hard to keep their heads above water that they do not have time to assist others.

One business owner I know had this to say about being a role model: "Role model? What would I look like being a role model to someone? I need a role model myself."

## 29

---

# *Survival Strategies for the MBE*

*We are troubled on every side, yet not distressed; we are per-
plexed, but not in despair;*
—II Corinthians 4:8

T his book was written in an effort to help black businesses get started and survive in a challenging business environment. Special programs meant to assist minority businesses are often structured in ways that cause more
problems than benefits. It is tough to know how to use these
special programs to your advantage.

There are many programs, and all of them are suppos-
edly designed to help minority businesses. Your objective is
for your business to survive and thrive. Keep this objective
in mind and use these strategies that follow to avoid the
pitfalls of depending too heavily on special programs.

## *Survival Strategies*

**1) Consider yourself a business first and a minority busi-
ness second.** Your business should be ready to be competitive with any other business in the markets in which you

compete. You should prepare yourself like any other business. You must have a product that people want, a marketing strategy to sell your product and a customer service system to keep the customers you get. Concentrate on your business. Don't become overly concerned with the color of your skin. Some people will do business with you while others never will.

**2) Do not use the term minority business in marketing material.** You want to choose when you market your MBE status. If being a minority business is not an advantage to your product then leave it out of your marketing material. There are many other ways to let people know that you are a minority business.

For example, you might mention your MBE status in a letter to a client who may find your MBE status important. People have preconceived notions about minority businesses, and you do not want to be judged before you get the chance to prove yourself.

**3) Join minority business groups in your area.** These groups will be a good source of support and business information. Many local groups act collectively to influence government legislation affecting minority businesses. Minority business groups often hold networking sessions, education seminars and legislative updates to improve the exposure of black businesses. Joining organizations of this type will give you a sense of support. You can share your ideas and benefit from the ideas of others on the development of small businesses.

**4) Take advantage of all special programs that will help your business.** There are many special programs for minority businesses. Find the programs that will help your business and use them. These programs are in place to improve opportunities for minority business owners who are serious about their business. Use these programs as a source to make your company stronger. Make sure the terms of the program will not negatively impact your business.

**5) Do not allow yourself to be limited to minority set-asides projects.** Your company should actively pursue any business that you can complete in a quality fashion. Use the set-asides to gain access to both capital and new customers. Then market aggressively to get non-set-aside business. Until your customer selects you based on your product, service, or relationship, you are not ready to compete.

Ask yourself this question: If I were not a minority, would I get this business? If the answer is yes, you are on your way to developing a long-term business venture. **If the perception is that you are only interested in set-aside projects, you will never get respect in the marketplace.**

**6) Stay informed about current business trends and opportunities by using mass media.** New business strategies and innovations are being developed constantly. You can find new ideas and ways of doing things from the experience of other businesses. Find various sources of information that are relevant to your business. Information from magazines like *Black Enterprise, Fortune, Success, Inc.* and newspapers like *The Wall Street Journal* will keep you informed on general business issues. CNN and CNBC are television news networks that are also good sources of current business information.

A morning of listening to your local National Public Radio station (NPR) will keep you well-informed about world news events. Visit your favorite book store periodically and browse in the business section. Look for books that may be helpful in the development of your business. You have to stay informed about what is going on in the business world. Find the information sources that best fit your taste, lifestyle, and personal budget. What ever the source or the media, keep yourself well-informed.

If the playing field were level, we would not need special

programs for minority businesses. We should continue to push for better access and a more fair environment. Improving our image will take time and effort and should be a top priority of every minority business owner.

Equality is not here yet nor will it be here in the near future. My businesses participate in special programs for minorities, and I encourage you to do the same. But your company should go after **any** business that fits its skills. Make your decisions about what business to go after based on your ability to provide a quality job. This approach will keep you in business and help you to gain respect.

# *Conclusion*

## *The 10 Dream Killers*

*T*his entire book has outlined the path to success for black entrepreneurs. The strategies, stories, and outlines presented here will make your business better, stronger and more competitive. Be aware that knowing the basics will not be enough. Throughout the text, I have suggested solutions that will help you to deal with the particular barriers that black business owners face. The difficulties blacks experience in business are hard to quantify or even state in simple terms.

A general message stated in many different ways emerged from my experiences, research, and interviews. I have taken this input and summarized it into ten major points—The Ten Dream Killers. Beyond the basics, these ten points are the essence of what will make or break your business.

Consider this list and be sure that you and your company do not fall prey to these business killers. The killers can often remain hidden until it is too late. Keep your eyes open and your business growing.

**1) Looking for racism and not relationships.** Racism is a fact of life. Many business owners spend too much time and energy blaming racism for poor business conditions. This attitude prevents attempts to build important relationships that could secure your business' success. Every white person is not racist. Most whites make decisions just like we do. They buy from who they know, trust, and like.

You must build relationships based on the abilities of your business. Some people call it social marketing. You must link yourself to any group that can help your business. Chambers of commerce, rotary clubs, and industry groups are good organizations to consider. Do not ignore racism, but do not let it stop you from moving forward.

**2) Playing the waiting game.** Procrastination steals the dreams of would be African-American business owners. Many wait out of fear, lack of confidence and complacency. Fight procrastination with action. Do something every day toward your business goals.

**3) Taking a trip without a map.** Many black business owners just happen into business. There has been no planning or preparation. Plan early and often. If you are running a business without a plan, take a few days off and get your plan in place.

**4) Reading your own press.** The ego of many entrepreneurs often causes the demise of their businesses. As people continue to tell them how good they are doing, they begin to believe it. This inflated ego makes the business owner willing to forget the things that got them where they are. Do not forget what you did to get your business started. Treat everyone with respect. You will need all the help you can get.

**5) Growing like a weed.** Rapid and uncontrolled growth can spell disaster for many businesses. Growing too fast without control can overwork the business owner. As the business owner adds personnel, without having an efficient system in place, quality will suffer. When quality suffers, customers go elsewhere. Create good systems as your business grows. The systems will help you to maintain your level of quality as the business grows too large for you to handle alone.

**6) Too many sociologists and not enough capitalists.** African-American business owners often make decisions based on a desire to help others. Although these decisions are socially conscious, they may not be the best for the business. Concern for our communities is important, and a high level of social awareness makes our businesses special.

But paying too much attention to social issues can put your business in danger. Make decisions based on what is good for your business and not harmful to your community. If you keep your priorities in this order you can balance your profits and your social responsibility.

**7) Folding too early.** Full of frustration and disappointment, African-American business owners often abandon their businesses before they really have a chance for success. Don't give up too early. If your business is a good one and your plan is solid, stick with your business idea. Your personal commitment to your business' success will make the difference.

**8) Underestimating your worth.** Poorly pricing the product is a common mistake of African-American business owners. They lower their prices in hopes of gaining access to an unaccepting market. Under-pricing your product will lower profits and cause financial strain on your business. Be sure you are pricing your product based on your costs and the going rate for your product or service. Set the price right the first time because changing your price later will be difficult.

**9) Riding one horse.** Many African-American businesses get started by forming a relationship with one client. Many times it is a previous employer or a local corporation. This new relationship means that the new business gets a large percentage of its revenue from one source. If this source dries up or the relationship falls apart, the new business is in trouble. In this case, the customer is in control. They can set the price and demand any terms they want. Be sure you get a diverse group of customers quickly. Don't let any single customer have too large a portion of your business.

**10) Riding a lame horse.** Doing business with poor clients is a prescription for business disaster. Customers that don't pay, pay their own price or just pay very slowly are often not good customers to have. The belief that any business is good business is simply false. Bad customers cost you money, use your resources, and can drive you out of business. Dump your lame customers and spend your limited time and resources getting more business from your good customers.

Being in business for yourself can be the most gratifying experience of your life. You can control your own destiny, provide jobs for others, and make a real difference in your community. You already have all that you will need to be a successful business owner. Desire is the primary ingredient for starting a business. If you want to own a business, do it.

Many people will say you are crazy. They will tell you that you do not have enough money, education, or time. None of this will matter if you really want to start a business. The market awaits your new business. Remember to send me a letter and tell me of your progress. Get started today!

# *Appendix A*

# *Business Plan Primer*

## *I. The Business Plan Outline*

### A. Cover Letter (Include if your plan is being prepared for a bank or investor)

Your cover letter should include and clearly state all of the following elements: Dollar amount requested
State the amount of money you need from the funding source.

> **Example:** Our company will need a total of $ 13,700 to implement our plan properly.

### B. Terms and Timing

State the terms you desire for the money you need. Do you want a line of credit that allows you to borrow money as you need it and pay interest on only the amount you use, a term loan where you borrow a set amount of money and begin to pay it back in regular payments or investment money which usually comes from a private investor or a venture capital firm.

> **Example:** We will need $10,000 of the funds in the form of a line of credit. The remaining $3,700 will be in a 36 month term loan.

### C. Type and Amount of Collateral

What will you be pledging to secure the loan? Your options include company or personal assets. Machinery, buildings, and personal real-estate are the most common sources of collateral. Tell the bank what the collateral is and how much it is worth. Collateral is only needed when you are trying to get a loan. You will not need this section if you are trying to get investment dollars.

> Example: The capital equipment being purchased will act as the collateral for the term loan. The personal residence of the owners will be the collateral for the line of credit amount.

### D. Purpose and Source of Repayment

State clearly why you want and need the desired money. Common purposes include the purchase of equipment, the need for working capital or the funds to finance the introduction of a new product or service. After you explain why you need the money, make your repayment plan clear. Anyone putting money in your business will want to know when they will be paid back.

> **Example:** We need the additional funds for two reasons. First, we need additional equipment to continue to meet our increasing volume of customer demand. Second, we need additional working capital to handle two new projects we have been awarded.

### E. Executive Summary

This section is an overview of your business plan. It should give present status and future direction. Write this section after you have completed the entire plan. The executive overview should be no more than two pages.

### F. Company Name and Present Situation

Give the name of the company and the present financial status. If you have any revenue, what has it been for the past few years? Are you growing or getting smaller? Are there particular items about your business today that you feel are important to this plan? Is your industry in trouble? Is your management team sufficient? Are you out of room and need more space?

Example: We are a new company that formed two months ago. Since we began operations, we have seen a steady growth in the amount of revenue that we have generated. Since our industry is growing rather slowly, we are quite pleased with our progress. We brought in $2,000 in our first month and $4,000 in our second.

### G. Location and Plant Description

Talk about all of locations and the plant facilities of your business if they exist. Be honest and do not try to make your business sound bigger than it is. Also give the amount of product or services that you can produce from these locations and what equipment may be present at the locations.

Example: We have locations in northern and southern California. We are able to do approximately $100,000 dollars of services per year from each location. This gives our company a total of $200,000 in service capacity. Each site is equipped with three color printing presses and two full size black and white presses.

### H. Product or Concept

Explain the product(s) or services your company provides. Be brief but complete in your description. Tell what advantages your product has over your competition.

Example: We manufacture and distribute a line of cosmetic products. The products include deodorant soap, colognes and body lotion. We have a special scent formulation that separates our products from others.

### I. Industry and Competition

This section should be used to explain your particular industry and your competitors. You may want to give a feel for the size of the market. Use total dollars in sales or number of companies selling similar products. You only have to include the market in which you plan to participate. Give an idea of the status of the general market. Is it new and growing? Or is your market more established and stable? Again be brief but complete. You will have time later in the plan to give more detail.

**Example:** We are in the corporate training consulting industry. The industry has many competitors that claim to be doing the same thing we do. In our city alone, there are 14 different firms. The market is an established one but has seen some growth due to the recent downsizing of large corporations.

### J. Management and Business Goals

What are your goals? Examples could be to generate a certain amount of revenue or achieve a particular percent of profit. Depending on your business, your goals could be to help some number of people. State your goals in numeric form. You want to have goals that you can measure.

> **Example:** Our management and business goals are to generate $45,000 of revenue this year and $100,000 and $200,000 in the following two years. Our management team feels that $200,000 is a level of revenue where we can handle our costs and still make our projected 30% net profit.

## II. Business Plan Content

### A. Products or Services

Describe your product or service in some detail. Include any proprietary positions such as patents, copyrights, legal, and technical considerations. Use your competition to compare and contrast your product against theirs.

## B. Manufacturing Process (only if applicable)

Describe your complete manufacturing process. List all of the materials that go into your product. You may want to mention any special agreements or advantages that you have with the supplier of your raw materials. Also give the source of supply and production methods. This could be a good place for pictures or graphical drawings of the entire process. Pictures are a good way of explaining a complex manufacturing process to people who may not understand.

## C. Market Analysis

In this section, you may want to give a feel of the size of the market. Use total dollars in sales or number of companies selling similar products to describe size. You only have to include the market in which you plan to participate. Give an idea of the status of the general market. Is it new and growing? Or is your market more established and stable? Mention any other trends such as a move toward the use of a particular technology or a tendency to use outside consultants.

Talk about your target market (the type of customers who will buy your product). Give all of the characteristics of these customers and explain why you feel that they represent the best market for your product.

## D. Market Strategy

This section is your opportunity to talk about how you will get your customers to buy your product. Your overall marketing strategy should be laid out here. Start with your pricing policy. Explain how you came up with the cost of your product or service. Then talk about how you will sell your product. Will you use mass mailings, telemarketing, direct sales or media advertising. Most of the time you will use a combination of many methods. Be as specific as you can be about the marketing method, timing, expense, and reason for each of your marketing ideas. Always state who the marketing is directed at and what you expect as a return on your marketing investment.

### E. Management Plan
The management plan gives the framework of your business. What form of business organization have you selected? Do you have a board of directors? If so, who are the people on this board? Talk about your key personnel (even if the key personnel is just you). Give their business background, education and experience related to this business. Explain what other skills you will need to be successful. Tell how you will get people with these skills. How many employees will you need? Will you need any new plant facilities or new equipment you do not presently have? Talk about  what work (orders, projects, etc.) you have now if any and how do you plan to complete this work.

### F. Financial Data
The financial section is the section most feared by new business owners starting their first business. Although the financial is by far the most difficult section of your business plan, it can be done well by a beginner. Do not let yourself get too frustrated with the numbers and different financial statements. If you need help, your accountant will be able to help you put these numbers together. Know what financial information is needed. If your company is not new, then you want to include your balance sheet and income statement from the

past three years. Some small business that have been around for years still do not have these statements. You can only supply what you have.

You must provide revenue projections for the next three years. Give the numbers month by month for the first year and quarterly for the remaining two years. Following is a list of financial statements you may want to use. Worksheets are also included to help you get started. Do not let this area hold you up too long. Ask for help if you need it.

Financial statements (three years to present)*
Three-year financial projections
Profit and loss statement
Break-Even Analysis
Cash Flow charts
Balance sheets
Explanation of projections
Explanation of use and impact of new funds*

* Note: Some of the items requested in this outline will not exist or not be applicable to some businesses. Provide only the information pertinent to your business.

# *Appendix B*

# *Resource Guide*

## *Suggested On-Going Reading*

*Black Enterprise Magazine*
P.O. Box 3009
Harlan, IA 51537-3009
1-800-727-7777

*Fortune Magazine*
P.O. Box 60001
Tampa, FL 33660-0001
1-800-621-8000

*Inc. Magazine*
P.O. Box 51534
Boulder, CO 80321-1534
1-800-234-0999

*Success Magazine*
PO Box 3036
Harlan, IA 51593-2097
1-800-234-7324

*The Wall Street Journal*
200 Burnett Rd.
Chicopee, MA 01021
1-800-841-8000

# *Organizations*

**U.S. Small Business Administration (SBA)**, Washington, D.C. 20416.
86 Regional Offices. Check your local telephone directory. The SBA can assist with special loans, procurement programs, international sales assistance, and technical assistance.

**Senior Corps Of Retired Executives (SCORE)**
Contact Local US. Small Business Administration (SBA) office. SCORE is a group of retired business people who volunteer their services to small businesses through the SBA.

**Small Business Development Center (SBDC)**
This is a university-based group that provides individual counseling and practical training to owners of small businesses. Contact your local university to determine the availability of this program.

**National Minority Supplier Development Council (NMSDC)**
15 West 39th Street
9th Floor New York, New York 10018
(212) 944-2430

The NMSDC has chapters in all the major cities in the United States. They assist minority owned business suppliers in getting business with local large corporations. They often have mentoring programs and small business education offerings.

## Chamber of Commerce

The Chamber provides a variety of business services. Many chambers have a division that focuses on small businesses. They provide networking opportunities, access to healthcare benefits, discounts on various business products and services, and seminars.

## National Association of Self Employed (NASE)

2121 Precinct Line Rd.
Hurst, TX 76054
1-800-232-NASE

The National Association of Self Employed is an organization whose purpose is to support the efforts of independent business owners. They provide various products and services that will assist self employed individuals with discount travel, healthcare programs, newsletters, and educational offerings.

_____ *Appendix C*

# *Glossary of Business Terms*

**accounting** - The principles and techniques used in establishing, maintaining and analyzing the records of the transactions of a business, government, or individual.

**affirmative action** - An active effort to improve the employment or educational opportunities of members of minority groups and women.

**balance sheet** - A report usually produced for the purpose of measuring the net accounting value of your company at a certain date and its risk to potential creditors. It is a financial statement setting out assets, liabilities, and ownership interest.

**brain storming** - An idea generating process involving the spontaneous contribution of ideas.

**capital** - Accumulated possessions calculated to bring in income.

**capitalist** - A person who favors an economic system characterized by private or corporate ownership of capital goods, by investments that are determined by private decision rather than state control, and by prices, production , and the distribution of goods that are determined mainly by competition in a free market.

**cash flow** - Usually measured by your profits before deductions of non-cash items such as depreciation. This figure shows the flow of cash through your company. It tells you your net cash generation and requirements each month, therefore you usually want to project it monthly.

**competition** - The effort of two or more parties acting independently to secure the business of a third party by offering the most favorable terms.

**consumer products** - Goods that directly satisfy human wants.

**corporation** - An artificial person created by law, with most of the legal rights of a real person including the right to start and operate a business, to own or dispose of property, to borrow money, to sue or be sued, and to enter into binding contracts.

**debt** - Money you owe any individual or corporation that has provided goods, services or cash without receiving payment. Or money owed to your business.

**downsizing** - A term used to describe the trend to make large corporations smaller (fewer employees) and presumably more competitive.

**equity** - Assets, minus liabilities; what you (or your stockholders or partners) actually own of your business once your financial obligations are taken into account. Also called net worth.

**entrepreneur** - One who organizes, manages, and assumes the risks of a business or enterprise.

**gross profit** - Profit after the deduction of all of the costs of materials or merchandise, labor and overhead but before selling and administrative cost.

**income statement** - A summary of the revenues and expenses for a specified period of time. It can also be called a profit and loss statement or P&L.

**industry trends** - Common activities or actions of participants in a particular type of business.

**leverage** - A financial term referring to the use of borrowed money to finance investments or business activity. Leverage can increase the rate of return, but it also increases risk.

**market** - The accumulated forces or conditions under which buyers and sellers make decisions regarding the movement of goods and services. The total demand of the potential buyers for a particular item or service.

**marketplace** - The accumulated forces or conditions under which buyers and sellers make decisions regarding the movement of goods and services. The total demand of the potential buyers for a particular item or service.

**marketing** - The process of planning and executing the conception, pricing, promotion and distribution of ideas, goods and services to create exchanges that satisfy individual and organizational objectives.

**net profit** - Money remaining after the deduction of all charges, outlay or loss.

nonprofit corporation - A corporation not conducted or maintained for the purpose of making a profit.

**outsourcing** - Using an outside resource to perform activities traditionally performed internally by a business or a corporation.

**partnership** - A legal relationship existing between two or more persons contractually associated as joint principals in a business.

**point of sale -** The physical place in which a consumer product purchase is made. Usually near a cash register in a retail shop.

**profit-loss statement** - A summary of the revenues and expenses for a specified period of time. It can also be called an income statement.

**racism** - The belief that race is the primary determinant of human traits and capacities and that racial differences produce an inherent superiority of a particular race.

**return on investment (ROI)** - A financial ratio that is calculated by dividing net income after taxes by owners' equity. ROI measures the percentage return the business is giving to the owner(s) of the business.

**revenue -** The total income produced by a given source.

**set-asides** - Something (as a portion of receipts or production) that is set aside for a specified purpose. Specific contracts that must be awarded to minority- and women-owned businesses.

**sole proprietorship** - The term used to describe an unincorporated company; the individual who owns the company is its "proprietor."

**sustainable competitive advantage** - An advantage one company has over another, that is difficult for the second company to duplicate in a short period of time.

# *Bibliography*

Bennis, Warren and Burt Nanus. *Leaders: The Strategies For Taking Charge*. New York: Harper & Row, 1985.

Blanchard, Kenneth and Spencer Johnson. *The One Minute Manager*. New York: Berkley Books, 1984.

Cohen, William. *The Entrepreneur & Small Business Problem Solver*. New York: John Wiley and Sons, Inc. 1990.

Covey, Stephen R. *Seven Habits of Highly Effective People*. New York: Simon & Schuster, 1989.

Davis, Stan and Bill Davidson. *2020 Vision: Transform Your Business Today To Succeed In Tomorrow's Economy*. New York: Fireside Books, 1991.

Fraser, George. *Success Runs In Our Race: The Complete Guide to Effective Networking in the African-American Community*. New York: William Morrow and Company, Inc., 1994.

Goldratt, Eliyahu M. *The Goal: A Process of Ongoing Improvement*. Croton-on-Hudson, N.Y.: North River Press, 1986.

Kimbro, Dennis. *Daily Motivations for African-American Success*. New York: Fawcett Columbine, 1993.

Kimbro, Dennis and Napoleon Hill. *Think And Grow Rich: A Black Choice*. New York: Warner, 1989.

McCall, Nathan. *Makes Me Wanna Holler: A Young Black Man In America*. New York: Random House, 1994.

Peoples, David. *Presentations Plus*. New York: John Wiley & Sons, 1988.

Pride, William M. and Robert J. Hughes and Jack R. Kapor. *Business*. Boston: Mifflin Company, 1993.

Schuler, Randall S. and Stuart A. Youngblood and Vandra L. Huber. *Readings In Personnel And Resource Management*. St. Paul, MN: West Publishing, 1988.

Sewell, Carl and Paul B. Brown. *Customers For Life: How to Turn That One-Time Buyer into a Lifetime Customer*. New York: Doubleday 1990.

Shanklin, William L. and John K. Ryans, Jr. *Thinking Strategically: Planning For Your Company's Future*. New York: Random House, 1985.

*The Holy Bible*, King James Revised Version. Nashville, TN: Thomas Nelson, Inc., 1977.

Wallace, Robert L. *Black Wealth Through Black Entrepreneurship*. Edgewood, MD: Duncan & Duncan, Inc. 1993.

West, Cornel. *Race Matters*. New York: Vintage Books, 1994.

Weiss, Michael J. *The Clustering Of America*. New York: Harper & Row 1989.

# *Index*

## A

## *Your Response Please!*

Thank you for purchasing and reading *The Black Entrepreneur's Guide to Success*. Now, I would sincerely like to know what you think of the book and hear of any ideas, additions or changes for the next edition. Please write to me, Mel Gravely, c/o Duncan & Duncan, Inc., P.O. Box 1137, Edgewood, MD 21040. For your convenience, you may want to complete and photocopy the Reader Response box below and return it to my publisher. Also, I would be interested in hearing about any particular issues you're facing for which you would like more information. Thank you!

---

### Reader Response

Name, Address, & Phone or Fax numbers

_____

_____

_____

1. Mel, my overall comments about the book are:



2. I would like to see or receive more information about:



3. Mel, does your company offer services in the following areas? If so, please send information.

a. _____

b. _____

c. _____

---

# Melvin J. Gravely, II

**Melvin J. Gravely, II,** author of *The Black Entrepreneur's Guide to Success,* is the co-founder of Infrastructure Services, Inc., an engineering company with offices in Akron and Cincinnati Ohio. He is also the president of IMPACT! Group Consultants, a consortium of consultants in the area of small business marketing, development and finance.

**Gravely** started his business career in Canton, Ohio when he founded a residential and commercial cleaning company (M.J. Services). This experience instilled in **Gravely** the importance of quality service, customer satisfaction and effective marketing. Seeking to broaden his business horizon, Melvin decided to turn the company over to its employees and pursue other business interests.

Early in his career, **Gravely** joined The Timken Company where he was responsible for the procurement of computer hardware and software. During his tenure, **Gravely** and his associates saved the Timken Company hundreds of thousands of dollars. After the Timken Company, Gravely joined IBM. He received the top performer award for being the top student in IBM's Marketing School. **Gravely's** responsibilities focused on ways to apply information technology to solve business problems. During his six years with IBM, he was promoted three times, awarded eleven times and stills holds the respect of his IBM colleagues.

Now a seasoned entrepreneur, **Gravely** has spent years researching the factors that create successful business owners of color. In addition, he knows first-hand what it takes to start a new busines. He consults with numerous business owners from a variety of fields including home-office based sole proprietorships to multifaceted corporations. He has written business articles for several publications and conducts entrepreneurship training sessions nationwide.

**Gravely** holds a BS degree in computer science and business finance from Mount Union College, and a MBA degree from Kent State University. He resides in Cincinnati Ohio.